Praise for *The Beautiful Tendons*

Poetry is an enrapturing process that intensifies the discovery of experience and only what arises out of this urgency produces utterance that is distinctive and honest. Here in these sinewy acts shine the mobilities of praise, the delight in the body's beauty and its surprises, the wonder of beholding energy and love. The poems are glimpses of sensual epiphanies, lightning flashes on the dramatic heart of event, memories from the crux of dream. Here are secrets that lie within the adventures of desire. Pursue them, and participate in the pleasure.

—James Broughton

Jeffery Beam's *The Beautiful Tendons* proves what many of us have known for some time: he is one of our most important and valuable poets. No matter what he touches on, it is always observed with Beam's precise and careful eye in spare, direct language that's as fresh as a sunrise and the sweet air of morning. Read these poems and brighten your day. I guarantee it.

—Michael Rumaker

All children should hear you, the universe glistening. The spirit of poetry and nature and Eros are carried forth into and for the future. You are one of the poets I feel closest to—kindred spirit in love with the natural world and kindred spirit of awe and affection to our own kind. Feather to feather, wing to wing.

—Antler

These juicy poems, at the intersection of spirituality and sexuality, leave me breathless with their erotic thrust.

—Edward Field

Though the work here was chosen for its subject—male love and friendship—it offers an excellent sampling of all that that's valuable in this poet, whose work ought to be more familiar to readers of poetry than it is. An unrelenting intelligence drives Beam's poems toward an agenda that's mystical, sexual, pantheist. He is one of Whitman's wild children. The success of these poems, and the poet's work generally, owes to Beam's consistent focus on developing a thought and allowing us to watch it move, grow, die without embellishment or gimmicks. He is the rare thing, a poet of depth and complexity who takes evident satisfaction in making himself understood.

    —Jim Cory in *The Gay and Lesbian Review Worldwide*

The gift to the reader is this: an accomplished, graceful writer sharing work from over thirty years, poems that sing from the heart of desire. Poetry of contemplation, lived experience and Passion; Beam's voice is joyful, carnal, and worshipful. "Take it, / and take it gladly " he exhorts. We are made richer by accepting.

    —Andy Quan

Beam's poetry, most emphatically, is not a poetry of gay culture but of the communion between the gay man and nature, both his own nature and that more general Nature ... More than that, his poetry dramatises a communion between a naturalised gay man and a spiritualised nature. Through the use of a poetic line that echoes both Whitman and Carlos Williams via Rumi, Beam combines the physical and the contemplative: sexuality and spirituality are fused in the perspective of the naturalist, in the observance of nature. Removed from daily urban life, untarnished by contemporary culture and clothing, Beam rediscovers the male body in the presence of itself. For this is what Beam renders brilliantly in his verse: the body at ease with itself.

    —*Chroma* (London)

The lyrics of *The Beautiful Tendons* do what poems ought to do. They brim with melancholy and love, a poignant tenderness and a delicious eroticism, the beauties of humanity and the natural world. They combine thoughtful and evocative depths with a pellucid simplicity of

phrasing. Like Whitman's work, they celebrate both the body and the soul. What a luxury and a delight to have so many of Jeffery Beam's poems in one handsome volume.
—Jeff Mann

The Beautiful Tendons ... offers a view into a poetic universe that feels simultaneously intimate and far ranging. The work rings with [Whitman's] same vitality and enlarged vision of the possibilities of the body, of the erotic. It is marked by the same cult of the "wild" mystic and the same generous pantheism. Many of the poems crackle with fire... In both the quiet and more vatic registers Beam's poems seem to work towards an openness, a kind of ecstasy ... In their best moments, these poems manage to press against such limits, of sound, sense, imagination and when they do, sex and soul, landscape and language manage to come together with a kind of glittering joy. He is particularly able as a poet of sensibility and visual response. Beam is poet of evident large ambitions and, to a significant extent he succeeds in achieving them.
—Peter Dubé in *Ashé Journal: The Journal of Experimental Spirituality*

The Beautiful Tendons takes its readers into a world where surface and fashion do not suffice. With a clarity that few poets command, he evokes an awareness of what it is like to live within a world defined by homosexuality and its pleasures. Beam is one of our foremost lyric poets; he speaks with delicate precision ... Beam is a very wise and knowing poet.
—*Talisman*

The Beautiful Tendons is a splendor, a beautiful tribute to the body, never sinking to mere vulgarity, but a real paean to the body and to where it may lead.
—H. E. Francis

The Beautiful Tendons: Uncollected Queer Poems 1969-2007 is a fascinating collection of verse by Jeffery Beam that combine sexuality and spirituality to the benefit of both. Beam has been writing for almost four decades; and any literary gay man who is unaware of Beam or his poems ought to be ashamed of himself! If anything, *The Beautiful Tendons* serves as a good introduction to this unjustly ignored artist.

　　—Jesse Monteagudo in *After Elton*

The Beautiful Tendons is a collection of award winning poems by Jeffery Beam. The poems are lyrical and metaphysical as well as sensual and dramatic. There is melancholia and love in the poetry and they are both tender and erotic brimming with sensuousness. Beam's poetry is of both the body and the soul. Here is a collection of poems that is accomplished and graceful as they speak of desire, contemplation and passion. It is Beam's experience and spirituality that makes these poems such a gift.

　　—Amos Lassen

These poems illustrate Beam's mastery of the resources of the English language to create subtlety in aesthetic quality. This is a mature writer who has mastered his craft and has considerable breadth in his repertoire. … There is eroticism, there is subtlety, there is imagination, there are unexpected twists and turns. There is much to be recommended in this high quality volume.

　　—*Journal of Homosexuality*

At their best, these poems are not merely about the oppressions suffered as a gay man or as someone queer; rather, the most moving poems depict the joys and pains of what it means to be fully human. The spiritual and transcendent trump the political in *The Beautiful Tendons*.

　　—*Asheville Poetry Review*

The New Beautiful Tendons

Collected Queer Poems
1969-2012

Jeffery Beam

TRITON

New York City

The author would like to express his appreciation to the Orange and Durham County Arts Councils and the North Carolina Arts Council whose support has assisted in the completion of parts of this manuscript. The first edition of this book *The Beautiful Tendons: Uncollected Queer Poems 1969-2007* was published by White Crane Books in 2008 as volume 7 in the White Crane Wisdom Series.

ISBN 978-0-9828074-3-9

Portrait: Jeffery Beam, Daemon Portrait: Jeffery Beam, Jeffery as Paolo, and pencil drawings all © 2008 Sue Anderson. The images by Baron Wilhelm Von Gloeden (1856-1931), in the public domain, are used courtesy of Matt and Andrej Koymasky. (www. andrejkoymasky.com). The Bathing House by Albrecht Dürer is used with the kind permission of Dover Publications. The flaming heart device is from Adam Loncier›s Naturalis Historiae, 1555. Vision of Dame Kind illustration © 1995 James McGarrell. Northern Light, Green Cross (Gospel Earth) © 2010 Laura Frankstone. Photograph, Enkidu, © 2007, Jeffery Beam.

Library of Congress Cataloging-in-Publication Data

Beam, Jeffery, 1953-
The new beautiful tendons : collected queer poems 1969-2012 / Jeffery Beam. -- 1st U.S. ed.
p. cm.
ISBN 978-0-9828074-3-9
1. Homosexuality--Poetry. I. Title.
PS3552.E146N49 2013
811›.54--dc23
2012026001

Abrazos

to the great loves of my life—Stanley Finch, the late Richard
Fitzpatrick, Alexander Gilmore III, the late Eugene Philyaw; and to
my brothers Alex Albright, Shane Allison, George Alwon, the late
Larry Anderson, Ross Andrews, Antler, Bob Arnold, Neil Bagchi, Ron
Bayes, Jim Baxter, my late father Robert Wesley Beam, Wesley Steven
Beam, Kevin Bezner, Stacey Blake, Robert Bly, the late Allan Boger,
Jay Bonner, Joel Borkowski, Bryan Borland, Jim Bowman, Terrence
Brayboy, Jay Bryan, the late James Broughton, the late Lightning
Brown, Bill Burk, Greg Cagle, Jim Carmichael, Bob Cavanaugh,
Douglas Chambers, Deepak Chopra, the late Dr. K. N. Chubb, Thomas
A. Clark, George Eliott Clarke, the late Tunney Cobb, Leonard Cohen,
CA Conrad, the late Roger Corless, the late Cid Corman, Jim Cory,
Reuben Cox, Thomas Rain Crowe, Simon Cutts, Ken Davis, Doug
Deneen, Stephen Dennis, Pete Diamond, David Deiss, Gavin Dillard,
Cy Dillon, Joe Donahue, Chad Driscoll, Peter Dubé, Roylee "Duvie"
Duvall, Miles Efron, Joe Eifort, Shawn Enojado, Ben Fambrough,
Michael Felton, Michael Ferguson, Jorge Fernandez, Arthur Finn,
Keith Flynn, Corey Sims Foster, Ed Foster, the late Wallace Fowlie,
David Frankstone, H. E. Francis, Timothy Freke, Jason Fridley, Kenny
Fries, the late Rowland "Jack" Fullilove, Eric Gant, Ricky Garni,
Alex Gildzen, the late Allen Ginsberg, Sam Green, Paul Greene,
Whit Griffin, Harvey Gunter, David Gura, Allan Gurganus, Robert
Hackney, Jeremy Halinen, Alvin Hall, John Hall, Eric Hallman, the
late Tim Hamm, Ross Hair, Reginald Harris, Warren Hauk, John
Hawley, Jake Heggie, Jan Hensley, Arthur Herring, the late Joe
Herzenberg, Joe Hewitt, Mark Hewitt, Josh Hockensmith, the late Lee
Hoiby, Jimmy Holcomb, Walter Holland, the late Darryl Hollenbeck,
David Holt, Jim Holt, the late Bill Hornaday, Andrew Hughes, Sam
Hull, Paul Hrusovsky, Jonathan Hyland, the late Will Inman, Peter
James-Thomas, John Johnston, John Dancy Jones, Paul Jones, Haig
Khachatoorian, Cralan Kelder, Randall Kenan, Irwin Kremin, the late
Steve Kohn, Mark Kuniya, Amos Lassen, the late James Laughlin, the
late Alain LeSage, Winston Leyland, David Lindquist, Larry Logan,
Rafael Lopez-Barrantes, Ian Lukas, Geoff Manaugh, John Martone, Bill
Massengale, Drake Maynard, the late Paul Mariah, Jim Marks, D. G.

Martin, Jim Massey, Joe Massey, Robert McConville, Paul McDonald, James McGarrell, the late John Menapace, Thomas Meyer, Charles Millard III, D. Patrick Miller, two David Millers, Keith Mitchell, Ron Mohring, the late Christian Moon, Ken Moore, George Morgan, Thomas Moore, David Need, Emannuel Nelson, Bo Newsome, Walt Odets, Mark Pandick, Rick Payne, Neil Patterson, David Perkins, the late Sylvester Pollock, David Preece, the late Jim Przeslawski, Robert Reid-Pharr, Renee Ray, Tom Ray, the late Woody Rhodes, James Rives, Mark Allen Roberts, David Romito, John Rosenthal, the late Ed Rumsfeld, Michael Rumaker, Damon Sauve, Sy Safransky, J. P. (Sandy) Seaton, Steven Serpa, the late Idries Shah, Siddharth Shanghvi, Mike Shelor, Nick Shepard, the late Pat Siderman, Joel Singer, Donald Sizemore, Eric Smith, the late Shawn Smith, Terry Smith, Greg Soble, Spiel Speak, Jonathan Statham, Shelby Stephenson, Fred Stewart, Jeff Stoll, Ron Strauss, Eric Streater, Steve Sullivan, Michael Sykes, Michal Tabaczynksi, Bradford Taylor, David Terry, John Thompson, Luigi Troiani, Allan Troxler, Wayne Vaughn, Mitch Virchick, Robert Walp, Sam Ward, Michael Watt, Scott Watson, Alan Weakley, Frank Webb, Robert West, John Welton, Fred Wherry, Tom Whiteside, Scott Wilcox, the late Wendell Wilcox, the late Jonathan Williams, Cecil Wooten, and Ian Young for their constancy, encouragement, advice, and inspiration. A special thanks to Richard Morrison for his early help with this book, and to Ippy Patterson for her later advice. I cannot thank Toby Johnson, Dan Vera, and Bo Young enough for their first strumming of these tendons, and Nava Renek and Tod Thilleman at Spuyten Duyvil for hearing these poems afresh and championing this new expanded edition. A special thanks to one of my mentors and inspiration Michael Rumaker for connecting me with Spuyten Duyvil.

FOR ALL THE DARK SOULS

WHO HAVE BLESSED ME

WITH THEIR LIGHTS

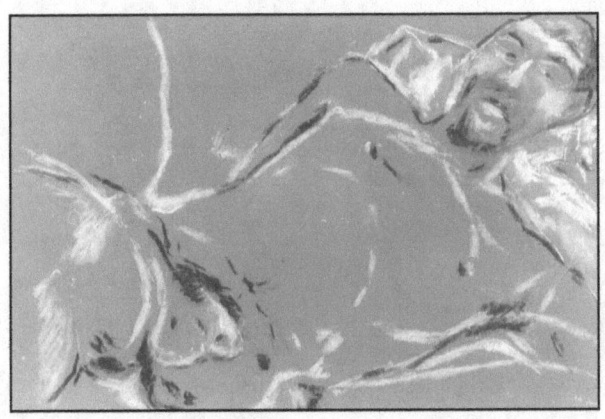

Who am I finally if not the long silent part of someone, the secret and nocturnal part which has never betrayed itself in public by any thought, word, or deed, but communicates through subterranean depths of the imaginary with dreams as old as the world itself?

Dominique Aury, secret author of *The Story of O*

Come, I will make the most splendid

race the sun ever shone upon,

I will make divine magnetic lands,

With the love of comrades,

With the life-long love of comrades.

Walt Whitman

CONTENTS

The New Beautiful Tendons

INTRODUCTION
to the New Expanded Edition

This new edition of *The Beautiful Tendons* expands from a uncollected queer works to a collected one. The first edition brought together fugitive poems that to me clearly expressed a queer theme or subject. Most, if not quite all, had been published during almost four decades in primarily gay literary journals, but somehow had not found a comfortable home in my published books. That wasn't because of their gay subject matter, but more as a result that none of my published books had been devoted solely to queerness, and the poems that ended up in *The Beautiful Tendons* had in one way or another not fit in with the particular focus or themes of those books. As expressed in the introduction to the first edition, the wholeness of my life and work has been realized through spiritual search; being a seeker and being queer have always been integral and inseparable parts of life. Every one of my books has contained queer-themed poems, but only a long prose poem *Submergences*, written around the age of nineteen but not published until I was forty-four, and eleven years later reprinted in the queer surrealist anthology *Madder Love*, seemed obviously queer from a reader's perspective. When my 2 CD collection, *What We Have Lost: New and Selected Poems 1977-2001,* was released, it included a large selection of poems from *The Beautiful Tendons,* which had for some years been coalescing but had not yet been published. The poems, as a group, expressed an intense Bhaktic feel to me, and I had sensed that they lent themselves together as a whole experience.

Now, with *The [New] Beautiful Tendons,* it seemed a good opportunity to gather other works from my published books (and the CD), as well as a few unpublished poems that I think somehow express my queer identity. Choosing the poems was not quite as easy as I thought it would be. Of course, there are the evident choices—but there are other poems the reader will find included here that may seem less obvious. That same reader might go to the published books and wonder why such-and-such poem was not included. I can only say that there were some poems that despite their subtlety when it came to a gay theme called to me to be placed herein. Certainly there is a queer identity, or at least the footprints left of my personal search for identity, and thus my queerness unfolding, that I feel in the poems selected—such as "St. Jerome in His Study." I have included "St. Jerome," for example, because of the acceptance realized through sorrow and suffering that the poem describes. Whereas I see the poem "I Have Never Wanted" as one of the poems that most completely defines me as a person and poet—the poem is a credo more than a narrative of becoming. So what makes one poem "Queer" and another not? Let's just say I've tried to choose poems that relate to love, the body, self-realization, and becoming.

For now, *What We Have Lost* exists as a selected view of my poems, at least up until 2001. The *New Beautiful Tendons* just looks at my work from another point of view. I could as easily pull together a selection of mystical poems which would glean my work from yet another perspective. I should confess here the somewhat impish glee I had in the organization of the first edition. The poems were not presented chronologically—a poem written when I was seventeen years old faced a poem I wrote in my late twenties, and a poem I wrote in my early thirties follows a poem written in my early fifties. I might add that none of the poems in any of my books were presented chronologically, nor were my books either. The arrangement, in *The Beautiful Tendons*, of almost 40 years of evolving styles and literary concerns must have confused at least one reviewer who articulated his dismay thusly, "This is awkward, unskilled poetry painted by a hand that would rather design a room with unmatched furniture." Luckily, his review was the only negative review the first edition received. In any event, I enjoyed his insult as I happen to live just as he described—my partner and I prefer eclectic interior design and live happily among modern and antique furniture beautifully, comfortably, and cohesively displayed.

The original organization of the first edition is retained in this collection. The poems added, though removed from the whole cloth in which they originally appeared, do retain their sequence, with only a few exceptions, within those published books. The new sections have been added to the latter half of the book, but I have retained the use of the poem "Diversion on a Birthday" as a last poem as in the original edition. [The sections of the original *Tendons* had been envisioned, over time, as distinct collections. As a result two poems appear twice in this new edition, retained in their *Tendon's* sections, but also repeated in other books they ended up being included in. An oddity, but the poems provide different contexts in each collection and so I thought it best to repeat.]

April 2012

THE VISIONARY COMPANY OF LOVE

And so it was I entered the broken world
To trace the visionary company of love.
Hart Crane

My mother was a good woman. From her I inherited my religious self; an intelligent, but high-strung Celtic bloodline; and the hard-to-shake part of me that sees, falsely, damnation in every human action. My mother was a bitter woman; in bitterness tenderness always hides. From my father's mother I inherited Grace—redemption's many-colored coat. Her "Is-ness," Shaker or Taoist-like, shaped me into a poet. When I was a child, we sang hymns together, gardened, and talked. Henry Adams once said, "Children and Saints can believe two contradictory things at once." These two women? The contradictions which have unlocked my Spirit.

Born in 1953, I grew up humble, redneck, in the middling-sized textile town of Kannapolis, North Carolina. One older sister (bright, kind, a life as one would expect—textile job, husband, children), and one older brother (schizophrenic, still at home, probably gay, unable to find the medium through which symbolic life and material self manifest). My father—pure, sweet, stranger to no one. When I was five he lost a leg in a car accident and spent a year in a hospital as a result. I never saw him in church except for weddings and funerals, yet to me he was a spiritual man. To my mother, missing a Sunday service meant signing into Hell. She never understood that I, intuitively, never believed in Hell. She only meant to save me from pain, and to ward off the evil spirits her superstitious soul saw behind every storm.

A gift: my mother's ability to rationalize her Irish psychic talents, and a rule-bound Christianity. She never questioned my own visions. She understood, against the presumed better judgment of Law that the spiritual world often breaks through in messages, signs, and symbols. Poetry's language. Institutionalized Christianity's greatest failing has been its denial of symbolic knowledge, or the misinterpretation of it, in exchange for worldly power.

Another gift: being Queer. Before I had heard of reincarnation, spiritual evolution, the One-in-All, I already knew about them. My life has been a process of remembering them. The soul, before coming into this life, chooses its circumstances. Transcendence comes with the Queer territory. In any case, my daemon brings me face to face with who I can become, my utmost possibility. No, this isn't an easy process. I frequently slip into the fires John Calvin built around the Spirit to keep the Body at bay. Some people make being Queer a political religion. I have found my religious self an ally in understanding why I am Queer. I use the word "Queer" because of its ritual connotations. Making something sacred from something intended to oppress and shame. I trust it encompasses, not just homosexuality, but all free sexualities as William Blake praised them: free from Society's imposed sanctions against the body's divinity.

The Celts, even as the early Christians, and as common in many pagan societies, were Pantheists, believing the Divine permeates all things. Children are too, until we fill them with myths of power, dominance, and shame. We are *integral* to the Sacred; participant in it, of it. Grace births from the regions of the Self where Good and Evil sit at the same table, drink the same wine, have the same desires. People, unable to discern Good from Evil, make laws in hopes of doing so. But it is the Law's spirit we must honor, not just the letter. and trust Goodness will find us.

Queer—a Desire Self, largely wrought. Some might say this Self looms so large because Society represses Desire; a material understanding perhaps adequate for political discussion. Lost, then, a broader spiritual view. Being Queer in Western society in this new millennium faces this Desire Self head-on. To couple with Death and Creativity as evolutionary forces—personal, but also human. The repression which feeds this Self is as essential to human progress as rebellion is, just as the Grim Reaper suspended above gay culture has also had its purpose.

As an impressionable and questioning youth there was a time in which I thought daily of Fire and Brimstone. At the age of fifteen I gave up Armageddon to embrace what some would call Sodom (later to find out through the research of John Boswell in *Christianity, Social Tolerance, and Homosexuality* that Sodom's sin was not of buggery, but of inhospitality toward Divine Beings. Fire and salt for refusing a welcome embrace). Finally, it became impossible for me to claim belief in ideas contradicting the "Sermon on the Mount," a scripture that made sense to me, and deeply moved me. I could no longer accept contradictions in my life when Queerness demanded affirmation.

I began, as so many did in the Seventies, to swim in eastern currents—the Tao, Zen, and Vedanta. In literature, I heard from Whitman and Jean Genet a different perception of this desiring world: "If I examine my work, I now perceive in it ... a will to rehabilitate persons, objects and feelings reputedly vile ... Without confusing them, it accepts them all, beings and things in their equal nakedness." (Genet) I learned I am not evil. I am It as You are It as We are It. "It" welcomes us into this world in order for Divinity to manifest. Rumi's beloved friend and teacher, Shams of Tabriz, exclaimed to his murderers, "There is only God. You are God!"

I found, then, a species of mysticism, practical and ecstatic, defined by Poetry, Pantheism, Gnosticism (wisdom in process, not just believed)—Queer. The Bhakti Path. The Path of Love. A poet's way, inhabited already by Whitman, Dickinson, Kabir, Mirabai, St. John of the Cross, and Rilke. I was born outside the city gates desiring the love of men, and born a poet—one with a mystical bent at that. The outsider sees with an eye washed clean of allegiances. I learned to fend for myself—the dominant law becoming revealed as arbitrary and relative. The outsider must work harder to define him or herself. Being Queer, I was either to go under, or find voices in religion and the arts that could reaffirm the One-in-All, the Body as Temple. I had finally to realize that on my own I could only do so much. A surrender of sorts had to take place before I could truly know myself. In the Divine I found a source of strength against oppression, and an understanding as to why suffering exists. This is an ongoing process. One in which I am still learning to participate. Poet James Broughton once declared, "God is my Beloved / God and I are lovers / He lifts me in tidal embraces / that turn the world on end."

Rilke once observed that angels and muses inspire poets, but I have acknowledged Federico Garcia Lorca's source of inspiration as my own: the *duende*. A force integrating both realms. A Gnostic force. A Queer energy:

> *Not a concept ... not in the throat; the* duende *surges up from the souls of the feet ... it is not a matter of ability, but of real, live form; of blood; of ancient culture; of creative action ... (it) is in fact the spirit of the earth ... The* duende *likes the edges of things.*

Society didn't have a chance with me. At my first thought of manly affection (and when was that? In the womb? Before birth?) my soul self would accept no other form of earthly beloved. My material self, at times of threat, has tried to live otherwise—for physical protection, but my soul force in me, the Queer *duende*, cannot be repressed. Divinity Full, it senses as Doris Lessing observes,

> *There is no 'I' here, can only be the 'we' of equals and colleagues ... We are the visible and evident aspects of a whole we share, that we all go to form ... Only manifestations of what we all are at different times, according to how these needs are pulled out of us ... What I am at the moment I am that.*

I can't see an anthropomorphic God (or Goddess) manipulating poor little Humanity. I see our lives afire with procreative energy; Jesus, the Buddha, Mohammed, Gandhi, as Enlightened Ones of particularly concentrated power, appearing at the right time, right place, through the process of spiritual evolution, to propel us on our way. When my soul, before entering this life, chose Queerness as a mantle, it chose to experience rejection and filth, ecstasy and transfigured form, the Sacred in the Profane. What else could a sweet-natured delicate boy do, but take up the sharpened sword of Love, cut off the head of Ganesh, and put an elephant's head upon the child? In Terrence McNally's *A Perfect Ganesh*, Ganesha, the elephant-headed God proclaims:

> *I am everywhere. I am in your mind and in the thoughts you think, in your heart; whether full or broken, in your face and in the very air you breathe ... I am in what you eat and what you evacuate. I am sunlight, moonlight, dawn and dusk. I am stool. I am in your kiss. I am in your cancer. I am in the smallest insect that crawls across your picnic blanket towards the potato salad. I am in your hand that squashes it. I am everywhere.*

The Naqshbandi Sufis tell this story called "Why I Did That":

> *One day a man came to the great teacher Bahaudin. He asked for help in his problems, and guidance on the path of the Teaching. Bahaudin told him to abandon spiritual studies, and to leave his court at once. A kindhearted visitor began to remonstrate with Bahaudin. "You shall have a demonstration," said the Sage.*
>
> *At that moment a bird flew into the room, darting hither and thither, not knowing where to go in order to escape. The*

Sufi waited until the bird settled near the only open window of the chamber, and then suddenly clapped his hands. Alarmed, the bird flew straight through the opening of the window, to freedom.

"To him that sound must have been something of a shock, even an affront, do you not agree?" said Bahaudin.

Being a Queer poet serves as such an acoustical epiphany awakening my longing for the Divine. John the Baptist states, "The one who comes from above is over all. He who is earthly belongs to the earth and speaks to the earth." The poet, too, seeks to speak of Divinity in earthly things in order to affirm the gift of being human—that place in the discarded shattered world made repaired and renewed—revealed not as a broken flower, but as the most perfect flower. This I have spoken of in a poem as "the poem / perfected / by its being / and me being / human / also that."

Acceptance. Surrender. A young boy, southern, "reputedly vile," raised Methodist (with all its beautiful loving forgiveness, its Satan and Eden), by Grace has revealed to him a Gnosis, the Poet's path. A blessing surely; a transfiguration welcoming me into Christ's body, under the Bodhi tree, into the Kaaba. Grace resides within each of us, whomever we love. I don't require that you become as I am. But if you require, as the great teachers have, that I "know myself," you must accept who I am. Allen Ginsberg advised, "Let the straight flower bespeak its purpose in straightness, which is to seek the light, and let the crooked flower bespeak its purpose in crookedness, which is to seek the light."

Trying to know myself, and accepting the person I find,

has taught me I am Divinity itself. It has given me access to compassion for others partly because I have needed so much myself. If sin exists, then the lies that society forces homosexuals to make and seek are cardinal. Our society calls itself Christian. How difficult it is for victims of society's misplaced morality to place themselves comfortably in it. How confusing to read these words in the "Sermon on the Mount," "poor in spirit," "they that mourn," "the meek," "they which hunger and thirst after righteousness," "the merciful," "pure in heart," "the peace-makers," "persecuted for righteousness sake," "men shall revile you, and persecute you, and say all manner of evil against you falsely," and "rejoice, and be exceeding glad." I remember hearing these words, and not defiling them, as some might think, by comparing myself to one of Christ's poor, but only thinking "all this happens to me, too, as a homosexual person, as a human being. Jesus must love me."

When I make love with a man, I make love with the Divine. I am your brother, just as I am brother to the stars. and the stones. If you burn me, this body dies. If you burn me, this body lives. A Queer poet, child-like, saintly, sees the Kingdom of Heaven in every leaf, every drop of blood spilled, every meal, every automobile, every homeless person's cardboard box, every bright mansion, every bird song. The Queer Spirit sees All-in-All in every act of love.

A Poem of Preface

In the roiling world,
the elms of all you were
anchor me.

Cyrus Cassells

THE MAN POEM

The holy writ
in subterranean light

Air
thick wet foggy

Our first Fathers
made their rage

and passion
in caves

Honoring bison
lion

bear
the sacred antelope

For clay for limestone
a hearth

This day ours
This day ours

alone
for men

THE NEW HUSBAND

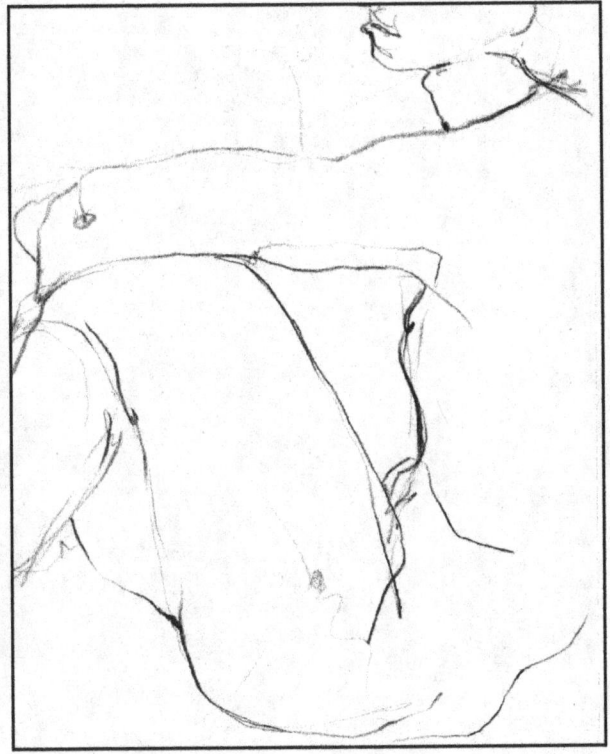

When I think of you, fireflies in the marsh rise.
Izumi Shikibu

For I am the new husband and I am the comrade.
Walt Whitman

Variation on a Malay Theme: The Changes

Cotton changes into thread.
      Thread into pants and jackets.
You let me go. Forget me.
      I've become another.

Many men show black locks.
      I hang bracelets on my arms.
Many say, Forbidden.
      I obey my heart.

THE SON

When the moon
whitens the deer
and sweet doves
croon
against the plow

with a deer's light
footsteps I'll creep
next to the hunter's
fire.
The son

they forgot.
Who, too,
knows how to fire
a primal urge.
Who, too,

from the coral woods
by the camp fire dances
into
the circular
light.

SELF-PORTRAIT

1

I drew it
coarse
I drew it with a lean
toward something
cross

I struck it with an antler
and a tail

I brushed it fine
then began
the spell

This image wiry
faintly huge
emblematic
strange

evokes the falling timber
round the house

In the fireplace
on the panel
two bonfires roar

I give them
each
a portion
of my heart

2

I think it odd
almond eyes
gleaming

Turn to take the kettle from the fire
A tea-cup full

A yellow-flash
The lamp and my throat
shudder

3

By morning
it has spoken
black and whistling

A strange hand
takes pen

I name you friend

THE TISSUE

For Alexander

The way you entered me
the first time
slew me   stuck in my craw
so I could not escape
did not want to
The hard bend in your sex
an alien visitor
throwing me open
We knew each other from another life
another time
as if the spirit
could not release the secret
until the body had been rent

My life exploded
a nova   then collapsed
into Desire's black hole
where all things slid away into
emptiness   Where fullness
became not sex
but word-rhythm
between us   Trying to say
what we felt   and failing
Trying to feel what we knew
but kneeling

So you have gone
and it's not that first entering that binds me
but the release
How you were born into this world
with my dead son's soul from this life
my wife's from another
my husband's from another
my mother my father my enemy my ally

So I cannot escape you

Lament

Eugene Philyaw
1953-1992

There was a man whose green terror,
whose rabid love, rolled, coalesced, trembled
in the small of his back.

In that silence,
that cleaved treasure, I would
place my hand. I would
feel his heart beating.

I came to you in your sleep
spoke to you of some
thing dire and consequential
Something like a sun boiling in a pot
A soup even the gods would hesitate to eat
What never left us was the wind
your voice
when from the tent
your head appeared
The blue mottle of your coat against
your black skin
I knew your
face was full of love
Each time I turned
I wondered
at my fear
Beside you
tall palms burnished in the sun
A fragrant answer to my
surrendering cheer

There was a man whose fearsome body
without reluctance or wish, in a dry
moment, or when his kiss
leveled me to the earth,
would strike me with his sinewy
skin, a baby's cry and glistening dribble.

You go off with my life
With the perfume odor from your wrists
a pendant around my neck
you go from me

I have no regrets
If the dark was more handsome than doors
I would forsake one
for the other
But I forsake nothing

Do not breathe sadly
The cactus blooms
odorless as fingers
They unwrap the loneliness
of your distance
You go from me

But the blackness of your skin is a balm
The lamp burns
Every time the clock strikes the hour
your feet come one step closer
to this room
Here already your shadow sleeps

◩

There was a man whose coppery voice
anguished and exalted me.
Who left his words hanging in the air—
deadly delirious smoke. Who
one day died.

Where is he now? I still
desire him. As God desired
the bloom of mold to begin.

THE WHITE ROOM: OCRACOKE

In the white room in the island cottage
we lay naked under the bare bulb.
The day slips by us as a white breeze
blows across our chests from the dormer window.

Only a bed, a table, the white shelf
stacked with few belongings,
while outside night draws the last
boats to anchor.

Water. Water.
The marsh ibis stamps her black feet in it.
The lighthouse beam shivers through the window.

I run a comb through my hair.
The live oak burns.
Roots and claws.
Roots and claws.

Two Loves

This is my lesson in humility.
My lesson in grief.
My lesson in the cruelty of the human heart, my own.
Trudging through deep southern snow:
finding both of your faces frozen in the white.
Sparrows still singing in the shrubbery.

I could not say it then.
I cannot say it now.
My heart split in two.
A tree limb weighted by ice.
A white quiet and protective.
A white dangerously warm.
My hands spiritless in the drifts.

Why do birds continue to sing?

SONG FOR A BIRTHDAY: *Calycanthus floridus*

This the month
when the dying God revives, Winter's fires
smothering Spring's flames, all
tumbling into Summer's thickening

In the air Love's green nobility

Such melon anguish the sweet shrub makes
Its multi-cupped flowers opening
Little lotuses at the wood's edge
A remedy
to slay Winter darkness

and in the air Love's green nobility
Love's   bright   coy   God

THE OBSERVATIONS

In fern leaves shattered by drought your half-smile
Self-conscious sweet thirsty yearning

Yellow your smooth skin black hairs' exclamations

Your cruel heart teaching me to laugh grieve love the night
sleep in mist

Lament and Song

Tunney Cobb
January 19, 1953-December 14, 1993

LAMENT

For every gray stone
alive with moss and left
unturned by your kind feet
Heaven's birds sing

Heaven knows somebody
hears those birds

Heaven's hounds guard your ashes now
Shine their green lights
on a humbled earth

SONG

Past white past water
past the last word from your tongue
past the altered rhythm of your speaking
we come

Before darkness before fire
before the simple angel of the young
before the field of lilies and
the birds of fields
we come

Past the simple angel of the young
past the field of lilies
past the early and the deep
before white before water
before the last word from your tongue
to us love came and you our love
did come

WHERE RUNS THE SAP

All night I have sat in darkness
listening to bees moving near
trumpets of the Conestoga blossoms
the red-hot poker flower's fiery
wheels leaning towards an invisible prairie
The lover does not come to their campfire
to learn sorrow in match sticks and fading flame
He comes to learn abandonment's sheer cliffs
The bottom of some gorge
filled with darkness a hammer
tied to a dog's tail
A farmer can tell you of sowing grain
The lover of faces like amaryllis
dying of thirst

A Man Mutilated by Desire

After Vallejo

There is no place like the sound before leaving
when chairs shuffle their feet
making room for goodbyes
and the ants in the kitchen
remember earth wondering
where the vastness of caravans have taken them
Honesty frailty in the human voice
is a bucket of rain
floating with zinnia petals
the Mexican flower a fine cloth
hung over my belly
You prepare to go
tying a red scarf around your neck
Your throat a canyon
a blessing of water
The Innocents are there in their pink shawls
You can hear them in the treacherous air
the further you walk down the highway

A Wedding Song for Men

After the storm, silence.
>> After love's bath,
>>>> the toweling.
After digging in earth,
>> the seedling.
>>>> From the flower,
the Seed.
>> Through foul weather,
>>>> infection,
sleep, and waste
>> the Blossom.
>>>> Some call a lily, some
a vine,
>> some the rose or
>>>> sweet orchis.
For mine,
>> I name all flowers
>>>> and then,
one:
>> pungent odor:
>>>> chrysanthemum.
A man's flower
>> single
>>>> shell pink
in which
>> the peony, lily, and rose
>>>> sleep.

THE LOVERS

I know not how I came of you and I know
Not where I go with you,
But I know I come well and shall go well.
Walt Whitman

Do you remember
the afternoon
under the maples' shadows
in early autumn
in the aging arboretum,

the warm talk of brothers
just accustoming
themselves to their new
intelligence, that
unforgettable beauty?

On distant paths, separate
they had travelled, and now,
their soul's startling interior
glimmer insinuating.
How splendidly it comes to me,

in my room, in the aging autumn,
the youthful brothers, their
darkening glances,
firm hands held
together under

common solitudes.
and the simple reverence
of blood pulsing
under the yellow maple.
The mockingbird above them.

SPIRIT OF FORMS: A SONG

A man's clear bent dwelling place
O coppery green it seems
This peculiar grace vibrated here
Your skin's gloomed rills

I candle love
from two ends I do light
It burns with fleshy fumes and moth
A humming rouses us from bed
Light through the window
Whiteness on your hands

GRACE

Two men lie down together
The sky shivers a leviathan
in red water
As one rises from the grass
rearranging his body
blue wings
extend from his armpits
He flies upward
The other sleeps
The dark star on his temple
brightens
A bronze herd crosses a meadow
Water flows out of them
Flows everywhere
Distinct in the wind the sound of sighing
What grace the body
pinned in Desire holds
What grace in the subtle body

UNDER THE COTTONWOOD

For Stanley

Under the cottonwood you stoop, bend down, picking the loose gray orchid-flowers, asking what is this that towers with snowy arms and is a fan in the forest for our love that has no name. We have been together only a few hours and the cottonwood blossoms have been falling for days, waiting for us, as if their pasty drop was a signal for this long train of timelessness to bring us here. Your face in half-shadow. The cottonwood, motionless. The street, empty. Yesterday's rain left its small pits in the dirt, the damp remnants of liquid meteorites.

No wonder the cottonwood stands so still. The light behind your eyes reveals something only sea gulls moving in from lifted fogs can see. Your body is half-here and half-gone, opaque, and if I would touch you, you would sift into shadow like behemoth whales, all folds and hangs of skin. I could not find you unless first I would be swallowed. The cottonwood know this. Who sees us here knows we are her woody daughters. We are fish in unfathomed waters.

ANEMONE

For Stanley

The celebrated
art
of love
is seldom
celebrated
anymore.

Among gentle men
such as
you
the art is
reinvented
becoming a new and

rare flower, a
blessing
to those
who love.
Fortune
saw fit to

give you
me. My
forfeit was
the ice
I knew.
My gain the

fire
anemones
you bring. The
lesson of
your virtuoso
art.

Blue Winter Language[*]

For Shawn Enojado

Read about these sordid screams
felt shiny after rock soars...

They swim these languid seas
men would say
not for most needs

but for skin
shadowing vision
blueness beneath
                              winter storms
recalling moon

                 Who

How winter skin
                              behind shadows
always misting
                              voids language

---

*   Written Primarily with a magnetic poety kit

◩

                    Peach tongue
sing essentially from power
behind white sweat
these rockless dreams
me whispering
to my friend
                                    flood

                    Watch here
rain falls
                    drunkingly
over all

◩

        The telling sky...

Will moon
                beat
                the sea with
                black rock

Will rain drive
                sweet rust under
                sleep

Watch
                my friend as
                        mad with love
blue light
over powers
                        the sun

Shaolin writes:

Flakes rampant
Dropping where they fall   who knows
From thieves to you

                              Smile

I replied:

As Basho might say
Thieves are thieves
If there's nothing to steal
There's nothing to steal

I wrote:

The snowflake falls where
it will
The pine bough catches it

When the moon
full as the mockingbird's throat
rises:
snow on tree
moonlight everywhere

His whisper

blue as gowns
in rain

LOVE COMES

not silent,
        but noisy and indiscreet,
                rowdy and persistent.
He comes in leaf fall.
        musty earth in his palms.

                Held out to me
I can do nothing but take it,
        and take it gladly,
                earth being the one coolness
other than water
        to be enjoyed.

                The fact of the matter is this:
tomorrow he may come silent.
        Tomorrow may be love quiet as mist,
                but today,
his cheeks rough with new hairs,
        I smell furrows of new fields.
                I turn over fertile soil.
I hear burrowing insects, happy worms.
        I taste the gentle, crude, excavating damp.

                The stain of love upon the earth!
Stain of love!
        His sleep rattling me.
                His sunrise and breath awakening me.

THE BEAUTIFUL TENDONS

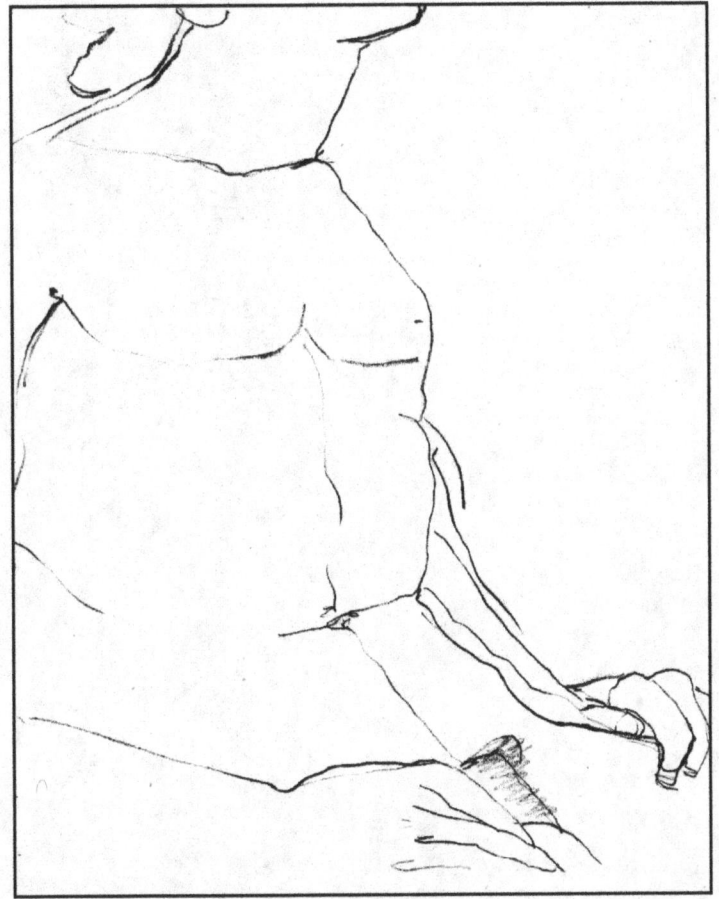

As the apple tree among the trees of the wood,
So is my beloved among the sons.
The Song of Solomon

THE BEAUTIFUL TENDONS

Do not hide the lantern
under the basket
        The night is grey

If you wish
        to light the place
        where you stand
        to see your lover
        and the body's
        stunning terrain
        finely honed
        its copper grottoes
                set

the lantern
        on a stool nearby
watch the shadows
           open every fleshy phosphor

1

The final spasm wild
        he closes his eyes
    jerking his body

A firm prick

Its tantalizing motions

2

A roguish angle
                the noble bulk
        casually
                in his hand

Hips swinging
                just right
How he rides
                this animal under him

        foaming
        galloping faster
                                faster

3

Hidden partially
by a quilt
a slippery cock

I stand before the mirror
shedding my clothes

Across the lawn
virgin bees swarm
the field of orange
daisies
Soon their sacks
distend with stolen
pollen

Tell me
Is that how you will take me

4

Suddenly
       he lies still
       in the middle of the fury
       his sex
               vibrating its weight

Then
     abandoning himself

5

Does it hurt
       He moves again

      The deeper regions
               yield more
     and more
Slip it in again

      On the edge of openness
      contractions

6

On winter days
          next to the stove
    he likes to expose
    against his trousers
           the little lamp

    exhausted from the dance

7

Merely pressing
                    against his legs' strength
The cool moss
                grows warm
The forest
                    helps
He begins to tremble

8

Summer nights
                    sleeping naked
Who is the erotic one
                    The lean monk-like body
or
                    The quiet moisture
                    collecting on the window

9

Smells of precious wood
                            cedar and mahogany
            clinging
                    to my body

My beard seems unreal
                        charged
with the right rhythm

10

I hold myself up
                    by two fists

We fall back among the furs

My belly alive
                    in the semi-darkness
A bolder gesture
                    grips the friction

The last drop
                    Pleasure

11

They began eating
                                Berries

Then thrown to the grass

the boys
penetrate

turning on their stomachs

12

A fresco painter
               this face
               fascinates him

    and the polished body
its slowness and ease

He demands submission
As soon as their breathing hastens
he draws out

Red and swollen
                    he finds
                    that mouth again

13

Walking softly among the primroses
he comes to young firs
vital subtle touches
               sticky and living
               so satisfying

To sting his thigh
a light hazel whip

               Nothing else will do
    His shoulders
    the ridges
    against
    his thistle

Priapus

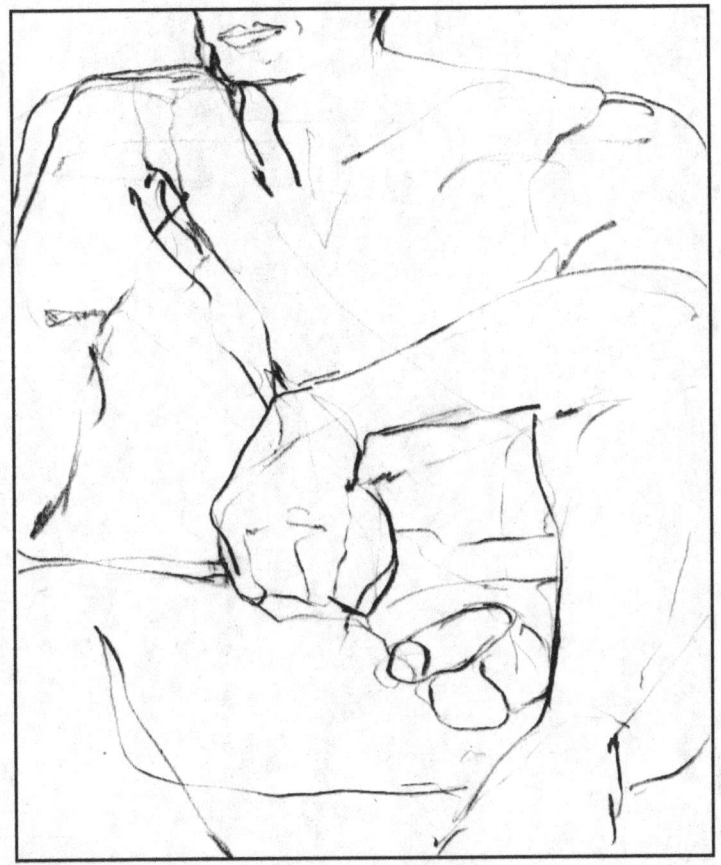

*All this and not ordinary, not unordered in
not resembling. The difference is spreading.*
Gertrude Stein

Poetry is a centaur.
Ezra Pound

JAZZ FOR DOROTHY PARKER

Why should I mingle
Love with sadness

That street glance
Broke me first?

and didn't it uplift me
Make me giggle

A grown man
Nothing worse?

Why should I mingle
Love with sadness

When kisses
Rule the day?

Or celebrate the heart's
Rude madness

Because he's simply
Away?

Why should I mingle
Love with sadness

I never took the
Curse?

and, anyway,
I'm all for gladness

Even at its worst.

IN A FAR COUNTRY

1

Let your hair
barely bronze
naked
tattoo in scarlet the marks
where the act
the touch

Beauty
The link
between
the cabinet of your body

2

Nights
lonely men festooned with red
Chinese lanterns
expose themselves

White bed sheets atop the grass

3

The laid-back mover

We were on the move
Visible
his hands
slowly urging it faster and

more

4

Me against the pre-dawn
The shadow

A rhinoceros horn
of angels

5

When the luggage was opened and
they had apparently
bedded the
romance

his skin
vanilla-colored

PHYSICAL LOVE

For Jean Genet

Can one measure
the circumference? Or can
one by palm and fingers
estimate the length?
Is it the darkness at the base,
the curls, the flicker in
the shadows, which most attracts?
Or is it
density?
Who can name its sweetness?

Probing the resistance, how can I
reach the tower, then
defect, slipping down
abruptly to the bottom,
glancing
in the shuttle brilliancy
of hair? It is
a throat
of melancholy compressed to
a purple wrinkle. A polleniferous
sack of
sensation, and rose.
To pass one's hand among the leaves,
harsh on the upper surface, soft
beneath.
The faint, dusk scent.

The fruit's neck yellows
as it joins the branch.
Then.
Handling the fruit.
Honey
moisture dripping at the eye.
One blooms gray with it—
the low-toned blush
from purple
to pink.
Oh joy!
The luscious pulp
so much afraid and so
courageous.
and madly, you take
the rise,
the boldness,
leaning, looking
down,
and elated, stricken
with terror, the sun-
light drives through your
dark caverns.

Priapean Hymns

When I arise
              my buttocks mark
              my sitting place

              Taking the smooth drink
              of youth
              I become
              drunk

Bathing at midnight
              in my genital spring
              I pierce my knees with
              thorny quince

              The skin's cloth brittle

              Wind
              blow through me your
              amber teeth
              I will remove each layer
              for a balm

You do not know me
              I am your daughter

Rising quickly we
              ask
              What will our children be
              Entering the house of penitential years
              The house of beans of
              hematite
              and corn

              We beat our hands in sorrow
              long as nuthatches

Winter
         we sit under trees
         in sleet and woe

         Spring now
         When will weeping
         end

Centuries ago
         ears of maize
         were called
         embraces

         One could wrap
         one's arms
         around them

We go to find a place to weep in our loneliness
         The garden path bordered by wild onion

I shall remain
         when the nails of the wall forget
         when the earth eats my dust
         I shall remain
         as mimosa remains
         long
         into winter

Redbud calls me son
         I answer
         He gives me this name
         for the prince who
         angers the wind with
         shameless promises
         spoken in the forsythia

I cannot tell you why but
        naked in this breeze
        my genitals roast and cure
        My body of three sexes
        writes its desire
        The honey bee
        combs my unhaired belly

Maimed and withering
        I remember
        love's inscriptions
        on your body of
        creatures
        rooted and flying
        Of ivy
        holding the stones
        together

INSTINCT

To see
the runner
in the cold air
at dusk

black
in his tights and
black in his
skin

is to see
thin rain
disperse
scattering

sparks
in the night-
fall town.
Down

the long dark street
he sprints
above the pooled
mirror-black

green-black
sidewalks.
Watched and
watching.

The trees
low
over him.
Their skilled arms

athletic spears
and
showers.
From the dank

air
from the
fog-ridden
atmosphere

he vanishes.
Night
surrounds me
again. Again

the chapel bell
rings in the
night-fall
town

and my eyes bend
their ears
to a running
man.

A WELCOME TO THE BLACK SUN

Be patient. How
can I be patient?

From your lips I sip
clear water, drops

clinging to mine.
From the branches,

your arms,
turtledoves.

From your skin
indigo seeps,

spreading over mine.
But from your being

proud lions roar
across the grasses

of my days. The fields'
camphor lights

ignite mine.
Mercy! Mercy!

the goldenrod cries.
and small rabbits

run through the grass.
Be patient. How?

When wheat
kernels pop even now

in the solitary heat?
and your lips draw a necklace

of rain down my cheeks,
mingling clean water

with scalding kisses?

On a Guess Jeans Ad

For Jack Fullilove and Alain LeSage

1
Spring in some city. Warm enough to move bed
Linens to the balcony. Warm enough, no doubt,
To lounge all day, wait for stars to come out,
Streetlights fusing in the river's evening red.

Pondering the question of his satin jeans
Some would call time well-spent, others not. Time
To enamor myself of the slim voluptuous rhyme
In his cool gaze, finger to lips, legs' sheen.

Discerning whether anticipation or loneliness
Excites him, I'm sure the pink spread
Rumpled by his dread but expectant caress

Matches the apple blossoms beyond the balcony's
Black wrought iron bars—two muscled filigrees.
Of course, his pose, all this, not to be shunned.

Not to be shunned, his pose, all this, of course,
An advertiser's ploy to arouse, charge the obvious flow,
Inner and outer. His puzzlement shows
Us contradictions we wish for; what choice

We desire. Ours, to insert into the scene.
He's beyond us, but each of us immediately remove
The jeans, yellow tank (merchandise), kiss his toes
(Shoeless to express readiness, repose). Sting

Red-blond shocks of oiled hair through our hands.
Sniff the armpit redolently shared,
Leaving only silver chain against bare tan

(hardly a line, solidly brown—if we hadn't guessed).
What price these legs, those eyes, these lips?
Could we but know his name, would he confess?

2

It doesn't satisfy
                          Oh sure
for a moment
                          he's all
you see

                          and then
those tight satin jeans
his naked feet
                          just right for
          sucking

What a puzzled look
                          half
                                    loneliness
half
          waiting
                          seeing you from
his cramped balcony-sheeted
boudoir
                          finger to lips
armpit open
                          alluring

You might just
                rip them off
those jeans
                        rumpling linens
while arched brows
                                (blond)
        under the apple tree's pink shadow
tighten

He grips the wrought iron bars
against your weight

But wait
                it's an ad

All surface all
                Lust and Madison Avenue

It›s him they want you to think
you're buying

and for a moment
                he's all
        you see
sunning on the Seine

ON THE HORIZON A SUMMER STORM

On the horizon
a summer storm

the rounded muscles of a man's thigh
bear me up
I'm digging in the garden

The forlorn dogwood weeps
I say
yes

It comes from some place below our bellies' surfaces
Our boots chant under the bed
bringing

the grey-footed wizard rain
the barking of his cruel hounds

TONIGHT DESIRE HAS A MAN IN IT

Tonight desire has a man in it
Sinewed thighs thrust against bone
Needs blue and agape
The heart's poison
sweet as blown silk
fascinated and singing

Tonight I would be possessed by him
By the virile rush of arms
a pale lavender flood
drowning desire
immersing the visited in the visitor's
torso of mild steel

Still and drowning
The silent swell of rushing thrust
wearing no darkness

The Bodies of Angels

For R.R.

are not unlike fish. Nor, for that matter,
unlike the shoulder you laid bare on your
carpet. When we remove the breathing
apparatus, the approach is the same.
A wind shifts. We touch an electric current.

SAILORS

For Richard Fitzpatrick

What one knows
of suffering
can never be put into words

Only corn-rowed paths
from farmhouses to streets
can say

Only the delicate
hands of cisterns
gathering rain

The jealous emptiness of glasses
A beloved darkness in roots
of wild carrot

Cities are its passion
Tall ships hulking through blackness
Bodies forlorn in tender armor

Quick gazes
mirrored
in the sea

Definitions

Honeysuckle veins arms taut kudzu vine
Wisteria crotch hair St. Sebastian's bastion in moonlight
Gardenia asshole home to the Dark Lord
Witch hazel lips figs on my tongue
Scuppernong wine dun cock tipped of oak beam
Armpits creekwater clay odor
Pecan eyes walled nuts for cracking
Moss hair
Honey-colored skin bee's sting in the soft spot
Emperor of Sex
King of Squeeze
Ruler of Hump
Sultan of Switchgrass

THE LOST BOY

I would be angry
But hear   my heart has
stopped

For you   ever harsh
soft as the whip-or-
               will
       sat stark upon my

branches in our night
vertigoed and greened me

Outside my window
                  still
nights light up

In bed I

Ache   arise

Arise   ache

PEA ISLAND

The last time we shared no name for it
listening quietly out of one ear
expecting any moment for the ringing to stop
I could have left
picked up my towel
stumbling up the dunes
but the singing wouldn't have
It's water's way
The sea's arms shape their own uplifting
The sun a table where
bodies crucify themselves
The sea gull has his place
The fish hers
Truly   our ways are our own
I come in and out of mine

CAVAFY

The mystery of splintering vessels
on a spring night
when pollen
a stallion's cloudy breath
stokes the air
and lovers tangling in the woodbark
of their breath
cats in weeds
is a halo permeating him
flush
and muscular
fanning inexplicably the blue flame
surrounding the room
the bed
the skin's murmuring
heaving forward
and back

His Penis

flower
of flowers
                    Indigo
                    cotton
                    ears of corn
                    morning glories
                    sunflowers
                    the Ivory Coast

The men paint themselves with rushes
to attract the wind
each layer of
pink
yellow
burgundy
indigo

a net painted with rain

His penis

a flower blooming in
dark mirrors
Yellowred
its mothy odor rises inside
a frosted circle

Geraniums nasturtiums grape-ivy
pour from its tip

The men grease themselves
with berries
turning their skin
purple and black

Gumming
their hairy thighs with
hashish and opium

THE MONK

I wanted to give my body the suppleness
of osier so as to twine round him,
though I wanted to weep, to bend over him.
             Jean Genet

His kindnesses to me are grandiose, although humbler, like raisins drying in the sun. He sees me as sun. I see the jackal leering behind each of us. But he tames them, the black moon on his crown startling their lunacy.

A red heart beats within him, palpitates, expands, contracts. I arouse him and his monk's hood drops. His shy sleep, regardless of the time of day, or place of rest, occurs under folds of tawny, densely woven cloth with a dull sheen. Two sacks he carries, wrinkled, of the same material. They syncopate the beating of that heart. When I lift them, their heaviness is mercurial, the contents globular and soft, like cold honey. If you touch them, you find them warm.

His kindnesses to me are grandiose. They whip an inner core, bursting overripe pomegranates. Forged heat of iron and steel. A slag as of coal burnt to diamonds.

He has a brutal streak which expresses itself often, but its gentle center manifests itself in a physical presence devastatingly erect, cool-surfaced with a subterranean rumble.

Under the monk's hood rests a single eye, which when amorous inflects translucent strings of light. I think of toads under damp leaves, the showy fringed orchid, blue-black, and the desert sidewinder pushing across sand.

Caught in my hand, we write a new covenant. A ripple of flesh. He, the God.

DickEssence

For Shane Allison

*I tell you the water here is the voice of becoming human
and it speaks in the name of all men!*
René Depestre

My dick's monk-hood drops
My dick taming men startling their lunacy by the black
      moon on its crown
My dick's shy sleep under tawny densely-woven folds
      clothed with dull sheen
My dick a slag-coal burnt to diamond
My dick eaten by wayward denizens of dark
My dick gulped entirely in spring by the gentle shepherd
My dick's seven inches slick with heavenly angels' praise
My dick's seven inches slick with earthly angels' praise
My dick a thousand million angels shooting from its eye
My dick hooded-hard held tightly by thugs and righteous
      orators
My dick deep into quicksilver/cavern/honeycombs oozed
      with caramel
My dick worshipped by a *coco* gallant tattooed with my name
      and mimosa charm
My dick idolized by a pitch-black *amigo* tattooed with my
      name and reckless charm
My dick venerated by a coffee-colored cupid tattooed with my
      name and seductive charm
My dick revered by a sweet *caffellatte amoroso* tattooed with my
      name and boisterous charm
My dick sweet-talked by an *espresso* flirt tattooed with my
      name and luminous charm
My dick cajoled by a *cappuccino* darling tattooed with my
      name and holy charm

My dick caught in the groovemouth of a gorgeous Caravaggio
My dick trampolined by a blue-black *caballero* his curved cock up
    my sugared ass
My dick's bass lines and drumbeats in a wrestler's turbulent
    throat
My dick a soft unintentional wink smearing succulent lips
My dick chorused by a tall tough's rippled waters on his satin-
    smooth chest
My dick novocained intoxicated erupted by a painted-rain Indian
    chief
My dick indigoed by a slurping riveter on high-beam steel
My dick painted with rushes made still by a merman's still-water
    mouth
My dick a side-winder hissing at jubilant bladed cowboys
My attracting dick wind-blown by Amerika's substantial sons
My dick burgundy for a Persian chap bound in jewels
My dick pounded asleep by my husband's throb up my tunnel
My dick slippery admiring from Shaolin dick torturing my
    tendered hole
My dick commended extolled honored eulogized congratulated
    tributed
My dick applauded acclaimed approved raptured glorified
My dick flattered buttered-up persuaded coaxed beguiled
    magnetized
My dick grandiosed honored exalted adored esteemed rarified
My dick Whitman's name upon it scrawled with grass blades
My dick decorated elaborated embroidered in the Hall of the
    Mountain Kings
My dick flower blooming in dark mirrors
My dick a moth fluttering between the green-grocer's and
    butcher's hands
My dick geranium pouring from its tip in the nursery man's palm

My dick nasturtiums decanting from its tip in the nursery
    man's palm
My dick grape-ivy lashing from its tip in the nursery man's
    palm
My dick tickled by a Nubian prince bristling my throat with
    · his flame
My dick churned by a slight curly-haired Sicilian under the
    Chiesa's shadow
My dick's sacks carrying soft/cold/honey/heaviness mercurial
    globular
My dick greased with blueberries suckled by the soccer
    captain and his team
My dick gumming hairy thighs with hashish opium
My dick a red heart beating within him
My dick between Hades' buns drawing charcoal-down
My dick between Hades' lips drawing underworld-white
My dick between Hades' hands spewing magma onto his
    red-brown chest
My dick Etna glowing red with lava rain
My dick riding the stag-God's antlers
My dick caught in my hand writing a New Covenant
My dick reigning before The Great One and Lucifer for
    We are the Same
My dick ripple of flesh He the God

LETTER

For Ron Strauss

I am thinking about Power and Powers that be and who
they are in the day of shells on some ocean where we are alone on a
raft
not fantasy but occurrence and someday we shall
know it when the Flood comes again but for now it is only to be
spoken and we will remember it desirable
the last of it will be spoken
between us when the Powers reveal themselves
Yes I am a great believer in Powers and know them and have known
them for
this life and others and their manifestations are sexual in the true
sense of Sex something beyond Body and of it one can feel even in the
screwed turning of two Bodies
One feels it in the cock and the ass and these are not pornographic
terms but the inevitable click in the brain which releases
convolutions of Energy into the vast atmosphere of Bodies
Of Bodies I am sure I have experienced them and they know the En-
ergy and
the Power just as the cactus goes without water and with it when the
rain
comes pilgrim silent and pure with dark eyes and the hands of earth
digging into Desire and Intensity beyond Light or Dark into the riddle
of come to me and I will answer the Questions and make you one
with
trees
Trees feel it on nights when the moon lingers behind clouds loveless
and emancipated and searched by
rabbits and squirrels by leaves and by the roots of things that have
known
the soil in their growth and in their Death

Ask them and they will tell you I know I have
asked them
So Power is in this room now in this room with no hands
handless and subtle blue handless and carried in the wide holes of the
stars
and they are whole holy and stark commanding the elbows of the
ivory night
with arms of iris
So Power Male or Female neither but the brushed incandescence of
the multi
sexual the Body made of Orifice and Prick made of Softness and
Damp of
many textured veins and wrapped tissue the mouth of the body know
this
its feet of apple
and of apple of iris there are many found Powers among the plants
and the
ores
Mineral is Power and so also Plant and in appearance though different
the
Source is One and of Sex
Ask of the Ores their beginnings and they are sure
Of Malachite and Cinnabar the First Stage and of Diamonds and Quartz
the ending
They are the same though colored throughout with difference
Of Vegetation it is the same of gaseous and invisible worlds also
Ask the Animals and they will speak it
Now for us then we have the Power not in the sense
of overlords but in the growth of plants and other life we are as One
Our Bodies know it our Cocks mutual in their juices our Hearts same
in their bearing
The tissues moist nipples quill of bone flax of beard circumcised and
uncircumcised the armpit and the eye the indenture of heels the
back's

high land and the nostril's basin
mouth teeth tongue scrotum testes frenum frieze of skin
Yes it is ours and it shall be spoken as desirable on that day on our
raft when from the Flood the Woodcarver takes us to his home
saying our Names

VON GLOEDEN

Inspired by the photographs of Baron von Gloeden

You only stumble on poetic truth in the dark,
in the light it is too easy to step around it.
P.J. Kavanagh

If you are squeamish, do not prod the beach rubble.
Sappho

A note
on Baron Wilhem von Gloeden's photographs

All testify alike to the discrimination between vulgar and heroic love in the Greek mind ... For the present, a quotation from one of the most eloquent of the later rhetoricians will sufficiently set forth the contrast, which the Greek race never wholly forgot: 'The one love is mad for pleasure; the other loves beauty. The one is an involuntary sickness; the other is a sought enthusiasm. The one tends to the good of the beloved; the other to the ruin of both. The one is virtuous; the other incontinent in all its acts. The one has its end in friendship; the other in hate. The one is freely given; the other is bought and sold. The one brings praise; the other blame. The one is virile; the other effeminate. The one is firm and constant; the other light and variable. The man who loves the one love is a friend of God, a friend of law, fulfilled of modesty, and free of speech. He dares to court his friend in daylight, and rejoices in his love. He wrestles with him in the playground and runs with him in the race, goes afield with him to the hunt, and in battle fights for glory at his side. In his misfortune he suffers, and at his death he dies with him. He needs no gloom of night, no desert place, for this society. The other lover is a foe to heaven, for he is out of tune and criminal; a foe to law, for he transgresses law. Cowardly, despairing, shameless, haunting the dusk, lurking in desert places and secret dens, he would fain be never seen consorting with his friend, but shuns the light of day, and follows after night and darkness, which the shepherd hates, but the thief loves.

John Addington Symonds quoting Maximus Tyrius

Baron Wilhem von Gloeden's (1856–1931) male nude pictures epitomize early photographs of homoerotic images: sentimental "classical" poses embroidered with costumes, flowers, tapestries, and amphorae in rustic scenes. Today the photographs can seem nothing more than kitsch, although some aspire to, and reach, high art by elevating their subjects into timeless, elegant icons of pastoral innocence, while challenging the social mores of their time. Von Gloeden's controlled lighting and special tints and filters heightened their romance. Their Grecian/Roman melodramas helped to make the images homoeroticism and rich sensuality palatable to the Victorians, male and female, who collected them, exhibited them, praised their ethnographic value, while sugar-coating their implicit sexual tourism.

Von Gloeden claimed to be a member of the minor nobility of Mecklenburg, Germany when he moved to Taormina, Sicily in his twenties. His wealth enabled him to pursue a lavish lifestyle, and to hire the young Sicilians as models, domestic servants, and companions. Some became devoted life-long friends and lovers. His presence changed Taormina from a forgotten wayside crossroads to the bustling tourist destination it remains today. As the village's rich patron he provided dowries and helped set up businesses for his models. Visitors to his estate include Anatole France, Oscar Wilde, Eleanor Duse, King Edward VII, the King of Siam, and the Rothschilds, Krupps, and Vanderbilts.

Jason Goldman in the online *GLBTQ Encyclopedia* remarks that for we 'contemporary gay viewers, the several hundred surviving images evoke a dreamy vision of forbidden desire, idyllic innocence, and a bygone era of agrarian sexual openness.' Certainly that attracted me to them, but I also wanted to play with the ironies attendant in these beautiful images. As in all achieved art, the photographs succeed, and sometimes fail, at many levels while offering difficult, complex, and even contradictory insights into desire, love, sexuality, history, and society.

Tauromenium

Greeks made you,
Romans took you, Normans,
Arabs desired, "spoiled,"
embraced you.
Von Gloeden undressed you.
Saw in your native eye:
sea, grapes,
stringent citron.

In the monastery courtyard
dry air cool breezes
at Taormina.
An arm lifted in supple repose.
Lemons and chiaroscuro.

Down the rows of cypresses
long bronze limbs
of young men
walking, as
trees, trunks
flashing in the light.

PANCRAZIO BUCINI

From the grotto
Il Moro
Prince of Blood
I see your olive skin
its film of dust—
the taut sleeve
shading you.

ONE MORNING

Cicadas buzz the rising sun
wooden balls clacking.
Monte Ziretto's meadows
warming from night's
cool ecstasies.
Breakfast of fig.......

Ointment

Spread it lightly, young
peasant, we have
blended milk, olive oil,
glycerine and scent so
your body will glow
softly—fields
below the village when
fog lifts.

SHEPHERD IN THE GARDEN

When I found you
in the garden
among rough geraniums,
coarse vases,
your flower, too,
violet and ruthless
stood out.

Beautiful one,
I'll not forget
that regal
anguish.

One Evening

Balsam pines sigh
under moon-washed
mountains. Villas,
wild creatures blinking
candle-lit
eyes.

MUSIC

I'll not forget that
afternoon in the room
when after we
drank the rime, your
brown buttocks set
the new tune.
How reckless it seems
now, but what bites
decorated your lips
then, and what
hard symphonies
we played out on
that lyre-shaped
rug-covered bed.

ESSENCES

When you held back
the wine, I
could see the God in
your eyes.
The mournful woo
of the cows intimated too.
and the lemon-rose fragrance
glistening on your white teeth.

WEATHER

There's a storm in your eye.
I don't know who
put it there, or what,
but a lightning bolt
just shot through the
window. My mountain
trembles from its
rolled sound.

The Baron

All the poor mothers of
the village know you.
The fathers proud
of their young stallions
carrying on stiff traditions.
This isn't romantic.
It's the grave's shadow
wrestling the body.
Hips swaying down corridors
of stone. Stain
of love stirring
angelic cypresses.

Flowering Apricot

February's got
a pink butterfly,
Prunus mume, caught
in your hair.
What an exquisite
loneliness.
What a shook
eye I got.

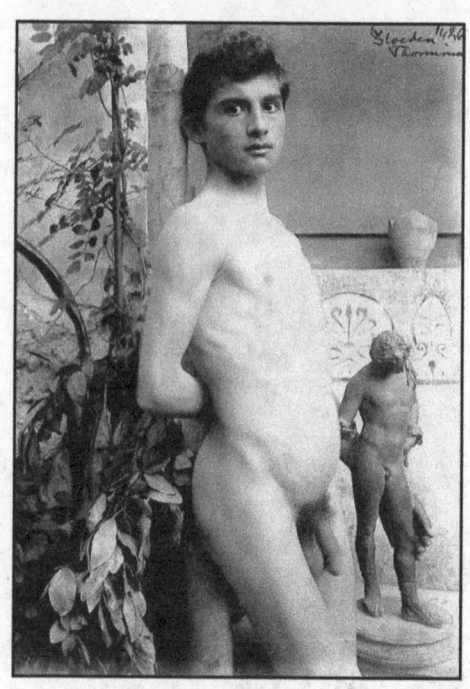

THE STATUE

The naive boy's penis
of the Greek statue at your feet
shares nothing with you.
Your bodies match—fuse
vigor and languor—
but the swollen
Kouros between your legs—
a statue can't approach it.

Young Man Holding a Palm Staff

A warrior of
palm. Nothing to protect
but the shorn innocence
of a necklace of teeth.
Lips pursed
ever so slightly.
Feverish as bursting
pears.

Young Man on a Log

Beauty has its own laws...
is the first step of a ladder
leading to God.
       Camille Paglia

That explains the dirtiness of
your big hands and
hardened feet,

the sublime uncircumcised
smoothness,
disdainful look, remotely
inward.
Liquid.

Stretch out your limbs,
I'll show you what
age and
experience can do
to waken
the beast in you.

Kouros with Leopard Skin

From what ceremony did you
come, leopard skin
dragging behind you?
Proportioned so perfectly,
Dionsyius the God, in you.
Savage me, dismember me,
swallow me with fellow
feeling. Look in my eyes,
Burner, the wall doesn't
want you. But I do.

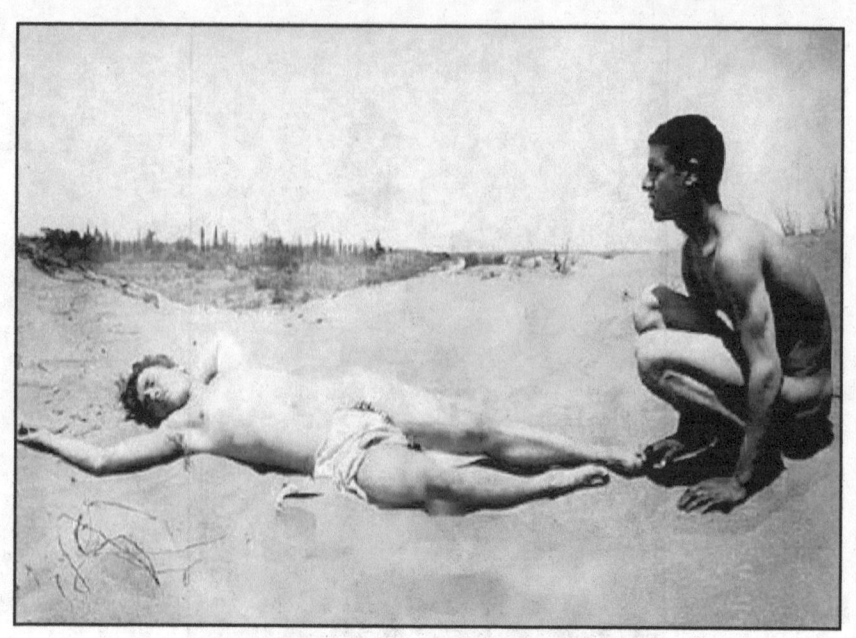

THE ANGEL

Ganymede and
the angel.
The sun bares down
its brass knuckles.
Angel, do you hear
his bones turning
to dust or to some
lustful, innocent,
earful of song?

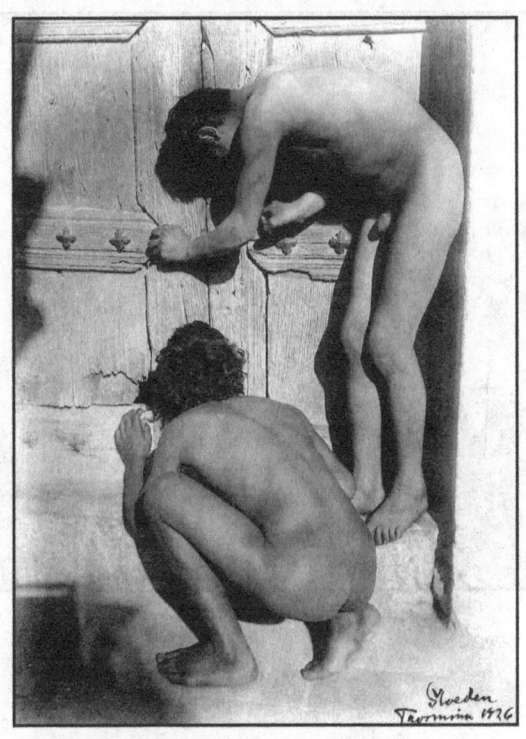

Two Buddies

A glamorous
scene, two young
thugs peeking through
shut doors
to what secrecy?
One smooth-assed lad
and another
bent to an anxiety
just coming on.

FAREWELL

That the world could
know such innocent nakedness,
your singular eye
coaxed
Mediterranean sun
to uncloud. For a moment
to carry torches with grace,
unconfiscated in torridness,
unmutilated
by knife. Boyish
and manly. Proud.
Utterly unsecret.

WASHING LINEN
IN THE RIVER

Bhakti Love Poems

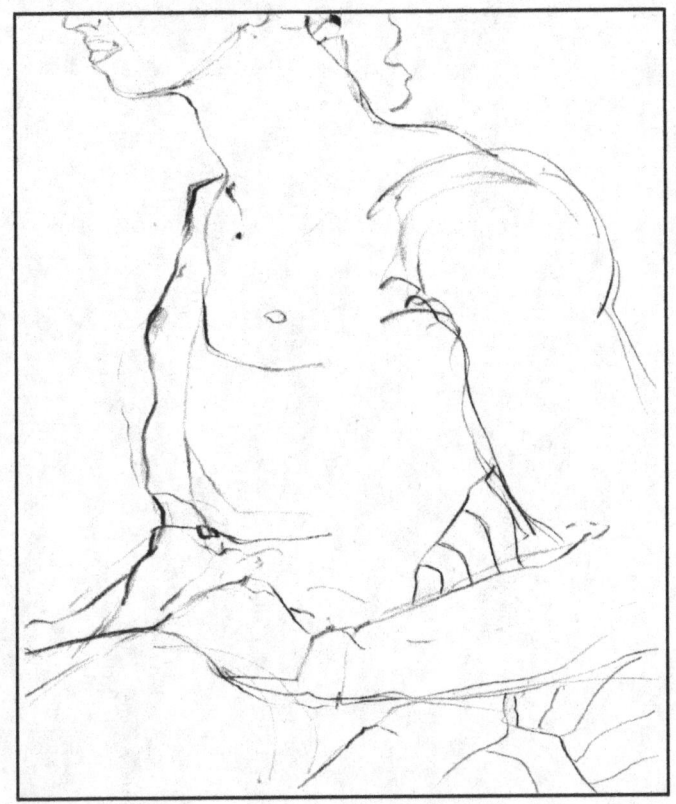

Love comes with a knife, not some
shy questions, and not with fears for its reputation.
Rumi

A Dedication

*For the Lion, Alexander Gilmore III
and in memory of Eugene Philyaw*

Desire
wave that shocks
with salt miracles and dancing
remember bewilderment surprise
extinction of age and race
remember greens of autumn
and my face
as I remember yours
carelessly alert
listening for the sound we listened for

FOR PRIAPUS

They shall celebrate in poems the eternal
decency of the amativeness of Nature.
Walt Whitman

Loins   be my oracle
Let the brown gleam be a bird
in a nest   let
the mushroom feed us
I stand before God
naked

Loins   be my oracle
A wheat sheath brought in at harvest
The sweating bell rung
when dinner is ready
What better oath than your brown gleam

THE SPELL

To see my Gods
                              to charm
                              their nudity
with
a word
          I assume
                              a buck's
                              sleek neck
steal
                              a quail's
                              small mouth

Troubadour Song

O Love you are the Soul of my Blood
O Blood you are the Love of my Soul
O Soul you are the Blood of my Love

O Love you are the Blood of my Soul
O Soul you are the Love of my Blood
O Blood you are the Soul of my Love

O Soul you are the Wound of my Side
O Side you are the Soul of my Wound
O Wound you are the Side of my Soul

O Soul you are the Side of my Wound
O Wound you are the Soul of my Side
O Side you are the Wound of my Soul

Verses should be sung with a:
"La de da La de da"
between the second and third lines
and after A "La de da de da da" the third line

QASIDA OF THE BLUE MOUNTAIN

My heart's a blue drum
newly stretched
                    beating

My shadowy eyes do
what my hand with swift
arrows does

The careless will never touch this
blue mountain

What a battle spear
when stiffened

Lover
I fear

What can muffle your
amber body

That Night

That body	tree on a misty hill
That face	fawn with dark eyes
That full moon	surrounded by evening skies
That hour	pavement ending in dust
That grass	green with summer's black-green
That night	coming over us with its breath
That sound	crickets singing at eye level
That body	me on the ground with their song
That body	another touching me with fire
That fire	round as the moon burning as the sun
That face	fawn with dark eyes
That you	speaking in tongues unknown and green
That sound	crickets singing in my ear
That body	tree on a misty hill

EARTHLY PLEASURES THEY SAY

My body's small
but look what yearnings'
hidden in it
Earthly pleasures:
ripe persimmons

My life:
as if it never happened

My death:
always simply smiling with me

Rumi says
Even though you tie
a hundred knots—
the string remains one

LOVE'S ASTRONOMY

I came here to recover myself
    to gaze at far off things

Your love found me
    staring at the stars

Stars came down
    sang in our bed

Their seriousness
    indistinguishable from mine

Their brightness
    indistinguishable from yours

TO BURN A FIELD

My heart?

A field

Dry corn
into which

lighted firewood
is thrown

BLACK SHEEP BLACK SHEEP

Black sheep black sheep
a secluded field after sundown
Inside the house a primitive
elemental
Fresh ears of corn
Husks
exquisitely
carved
Your waist I find now raised
To the left of your pillow
a purple cyclamen descending
Black sheep black sheep
a secluded field after sundown
but inside the house a primitive
elemental

BLUE CANCIONE

The evening's feeble
crippled
                            feeling
            my loneliness

Then
            a breeze
flowers
                        his mouth
                        his breath

His moist cheek

We said goodnight
Death would have tasted better

I FELL IN LOVE WITH

a young cedar slender
fragrant dewy fresh

Shadowed days
protected the thrill

No complaints except
those days

Too brief

THE SNARE

My black-skinned lover
whose only whites

his pearl mouth

Shaped from the pupil's
charcoal labyrinth

All eyes
                must
fix on
        him

THE IDOL

Whenever I see him
dressed in red
my heart splits
                    scornfully
He's the one who
                    with a glance
spills a person's blood
                    His clothing
drenched
          in mineral purple

ENTOMOLOGY

All I want:
       your affection

The rest:
       the earth
       mankind:

atoms
     of dust
Little insects

LOVE DOCTOR

My lover tries
to hide his sighs

Gives me health
or illness
The choice his

I'm fettered   a trout
captured

A shiny fish in his hand

The Warmth

Come close to me
as lizards do the wall

or watch my paper nest
crowded with love songs
hornet-sharp

I have much to say
but my name is silence
If you listen
I say enough without winds

I pass you
my bones shake

QASIDA

Oh you
whose waist
so slender
almost breaks

what makes your heart
so coarse

I give you all you want
I'm a lily
waiting for summer's
sun-serpent warmth
where sadness has no place

I talk to you
becoming drunk

If you are near
speak

LOVESICK SHIRT

They visit him
Grown thin
No flesh
No bones
Nothing resembling a body

Love's wrapped him in an ill suit
No visible trace left

MEDIEVAL SONG

With what cool eyes the noonday lovers part
In watchful bonds the evening light goes down
Goes down in streams of evening rosy light
The secret eye of Love their sonnet sings

O lovers weep for Love's silver sacred plight
The Vision leapt and poured upon the Wheel
As sadness draws upon the holy magic flood
and rides within the womb so red and deep

My soul is yours is written on the plain
Is sadly swept and somehow guarded strong
O gentle Love rise up and figure here
My sense is light and lightning fills my song

With what cool eyes the noonday lovers part
In watchful bonds the evening light goes down
Goes down in streams of evening rosy light
The secret eye of Love their sonnet sings

THE VICTIM

One curtain drops
            Another rises
The moon's
an arm band in
the sky   Darkness
streaks his back
with light down

What excuse can I give?

He turns away
How I wish to come near him
Have his love show me
something

A Flower Song

This white narcissus
forced in Spring
color of a lover
in pain
                Sweet
as the lover's first
meeting breath

Pale as he waits
                  patiently
bereft
        for one who never
comes
                Who forgot
how fleetingly

Beauty goes

I Write to You

I write

If I were able
    to *say*

the ink from my eyes
would fill the pen

          my fingers make

Washing Linen in the River

On the water
wind
spins
     a coat-of-mail

You cannot return

driven away
         by the current

May abundant storms
comfort you
      always

The Unobtainable

1

Persist for
water
        hollows rock
if for many days it
                        drops
then
departs
        A drizzle's not
abundant
        but soaks the soil

Watching myself
I miss you

2

You left   I left
Nothing inside me calm
Stars fell from the sky
Longing filled with dry tears

Losing you   my days
changed to black
With you
how whitely our nights burned

BLUES FOR GOODBYE

White elder flowers give way
to reddish fruit

Salmon
leap the water's high wall

You ask
"Where are we going?"

I answer:
The basil patch at home

Cool wind
                            whistling
among poplars

TREE

For Stanley

Your hands
                Wheat-colored

Your sycamore lights

THE ARCHER

You made me handsome and
a nimble archer
                          Not
for a moment
                will I stop fighting
A poor heart has nothing
only
           goodness

My arrow stiffens
                      Roots salty
        remembering the fens
            carrying me
                          to you

Qasida of Your Presence: A Song

For Stanley

When after a journey of no rest
and slow destinations
little is left in the communal water-bags
Only small moisture in the men's water-skins
The milestones so hot
we cannot lean against them
The feet ache with a porcupine's dullness
From what back stoop have I watched
you drift down the road
Your forehead a field
where a house once stood
I fear I might die in bed
when the sun is a stranger
Stumbling towards you I see
the water of your hands

BURNINGS

Don't mind a bonfire
of my words
                    Tell my message
People will see
what I know

Burning papers
cannot destroy the Word

Wherever I
                    stop
the Word lives on

Even
in my grave

PASTORAL

Old tree
        Dying vine
Blackbird

A little bridge
Stream   Cottage
Ancient road
West wind blowing

A thin horse:

sorrowful lover at
the earth's end

APOSTROPHE TO STANLEY

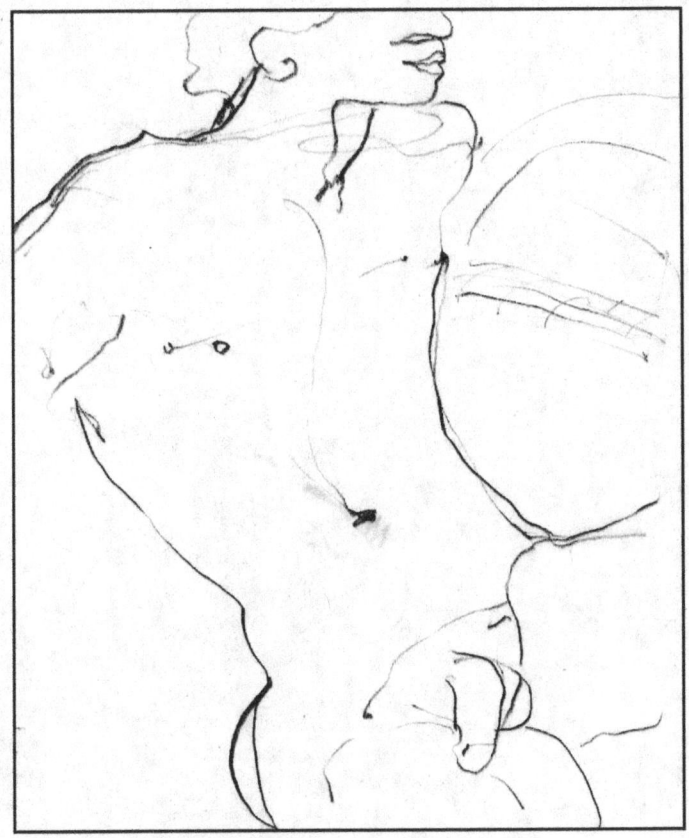

The Grindstone is desire.
Thomas Meyer

To live is to tilt with the lightning,
two bodies routed by a single honey's sweet.
Pablo Neruda

The Well at the World's End

There is a love that madmen know
howling in the night
like trees putting on new leaves
I will find it

These are a man's illuminations
A man's words to the backwater legs of manliness
The groaning hairlessness and hairiness of chests
Nostrils widening
Eyes targeting and impulsive hair luminous
The virile tenderness that falls
in gestures poised under
rough cloth

They were in bed together, the two men, yes, the two of them
and they heard with their ears with their hearts their instru-
ments of listening the first sound they had ever seen. Two bod-
ies rubbing together do not make it, although they contrib-
ute, nor two sperm in a million million. It is the sound made
whether separated by planets or separated by rooms, separated
by hours or not separated but merged. Whitman says, "Who
need be afraid of the merge?" and I say I hear it, and so do you.
Is it not the same as one hand clapping, your soul and mine?

With no fear of blood
I find you
so beautiful
kneeling

There is no tenderness like your body
in its pool of hot water
evenings when you soap your cloth
No tenderness
like your body

In *The Notebooks Of Malte Laurids Brigge*, Rilke says, "But, Master, were a virginal spirit to lie with innocent ear beside your sound: he would die of blessedness, or he would gestate infinite things and his impregnated brain would burst with so much birth."

What sounds do I hear in you?

NOCTURNE IN BLUES AND GRAY

The evening rolls on its smoky wheels
Its silence an unhealed wound
As if remembering
stationary   listening
for a moment the wasp wavers in mid-air
mid-swoon

Your voice from the kitchen
resonates in the door frame
Coming from dust
what armor settles us now
Only its surface in sight

My penis hardens. I begin to stroke it, thinking of the rough
bark of trees, the oaks, grave limbs of athletes. It stirs, emit-
ting an odor of cats. My strokes become obsessive, my sex-
ual hair humble, a triangular swatch of pencil marks in my
thighs, only a fine line up to my navel, my armpits shadowed,
my closely cropped hair and beard, ominous, serious, con-
tradicting the deep brown eyes. I see myself as all darkness
and light swirling. Magical. Unstable and muted. Capable of
spell-casting. If I stepped out of the room away from the bed,
into the woods, the dirt, the fluted air, my body would be
a tattoo, broken, dyed by the primary colors of my hand...
struggling to release a perfume into the world.

Every tree remembers his touch and I hang from them.

SONG

Tomorrow he comes
We will turn down
the five blankets the woven spread
the sheets those doves
from the dark places
the recesses his eyes
with their perpendicular fire
Green he will say
Green and slow
as cold snow whips our window

I'll give up my ghost
under his crooning
under his crooning

In the *Talmud* it is said: "To learn about the Invisible, look at the Visible." Lead me to a secret light. I will look at you long and long.

Mood Indigo

Stay with me and
I will make a drum of my heart
Light lanterns so
even the absent will mutter your name
Don't you see
I am lost without you
Lying beside you I forget all language
but your legs' language
When I'm full I don't need words
You are bread
your eyebrows crusts
of blackest silk

The bird's nest of our balls
Their warm bagginess and slim arrogance

After Love-Making

After rain
pigeons roost in the vines
A wet fortress their beds
I want to struggle to be good with them
cooing and damp in their blue tails

Your hoarse breathing last night woke me. Your mouth seemed full of ash, but you turned suddenly silent. Your right hand lay across your chest. Your left hand wrapped around my shoulders. In the moonlight I could see the sharp bones protruding from your shoulders. Those two small points are hooks and I ache to touch them. Will you awaken? I would kill almost to prevent this from changing.

How many nights would I sit beside you as you sleep, as your breath calls me in the darkness, ashen or clean? I am deaf beside you, because your breath is the bottom of a pool where blind fish live, where sound is empty, all light and sensation.

Your body, a scar on my mind. I can't remove it. I wonder how the human body could have come to this. Yours is a field of uncharted stars. The stars slowly drop down, singly and in pairs, into my view. Each star represents some bodily part: a mole, a nostril, a fingernail, the crease where your upper and lower lips meet, your capillaries, your down-hanging testicles. No wonder so many people fear nakedness. Just look at the spread of the body!

�(«■»)

It was not so unusual that you appeared when you did, but that, when you arrived, my life was an open book and still you managed to read lines unwritten. It was an omen, an icon, if you wish. Something to heed or worship, a notion to be kept close to the heart, even while washing dishes or digging in the garden. The corn knew it, the evening of the storm, red with destruction. The next day, the corn flattened, I heard the darkness of the unformed silks whispering your name. Within days the corn stood tall and straight again.

I wonder how many times I scanned the horizon, looking straight at you, but rested on a more familiar constellation? What has this to do with astronomy and the length of memory? I enter a forest. The starry field and the stand of corn point True North. I threw my compass away. I haven't been lost since.

APOSTROPHE TO STANLEY

Your chest unshirted
the sun preparing
a dismissal of light

Possibly
the possibility of its going
is of a light
we know not

and if we know it
or do not
Remember
Shade is the property
of the reborn
Its own bestowing

In coolness your body
You over me

The world's
blind ones watch us
never knowing
what the body knows
and tell

POEMS FROM THE GOLDEN LEGEND

(1981, Floating Island Publications)

Here we cease living and the house is filled with other and

Darker existences; we put on their lives and go clothed in them.
Edith Sitwell

The shadow created the light, but the light created the shadow.
Marguerite Young

AUBADE

In the dank cold shivering shade
the obsidian snake raises up on its elbows
and gazes toward the sea

My arms
are empty of you and blind
I remember last night's mothy wings

Yet deep in the darkness of my cells
I see the sea's roar
and the breathings of sand
The sound's so bright
I can hardly lift it

Across the grass
old women are loosening their braids

Mauve

There is nothing that can make you visible. Nothing which can save you from the oblivion of shadows, a plumed darkness, a young bird, sensitive and joyous. Sunlight enters the room and sheds plum blossoms on you, but the shadows enlarge and deepen. They fill the fruit bowl with damsons and the vase with salmon mums and roses. Where but here is the somnolent rhythm of the feminine, the sinuous rills of sacred heron eyes, so calm glowing like birth and polished whalebone!

The waves of light go out in ripples, they enter the mahogany of the chairs, the labyrinthine bivalves sailing through our speech. You are gathering beasts under your wings. We rise up, pale phoenixes in the dawn. We have been where the soul welcomes its own shadow!

THE SILENT SPEAK FOR YOU

For Peter-James Thomas

Every night when you are giving
yourself to your nameless man
you give yourself to me also
and a frightening pulse of love
sheds out of you like leaves
summer asters and sage
while a red-voiced internal fire
breeds its thin weeds
under your branches

I love your dark soul
your green brow pressing over me

Your body an open hand
filled with clusters of grape and moonbeam
white immense delicate
as the black dirt
smudged on your ankles
Your curly hair
a cavern I fall into
with no candles
seeing through your eyes
flame orchids
and the scarlet hum
of a red-winged blackbird

Although you may never be mine
even as our love
wakens the dead from their wide sleepy river
I will always be joyful

I will be a white handkerchief
blown by a hurricane's eye
suspended by a sad power
that will not drop me

Tonight the blue stallions of my love
rumble across your dreams

The silent speak for you
for you cannot answer

On Water from Wells

The bucket drops into the well with a long splash
I raise it up
tasting wet emptinesses
The ripples in the well-bottom
move in me
like the ripples in the red dress
my lovely friend is wearing
What grave joy she buries there
mounting the stairs with her floating muted feet

I can't say anymore
where light begins how fingers open doors
The withered man inside me
is tying his shoes   ready to go
and the first lover approaches
the well with his hands empty

How happy the grasshoppers
leaping in the grass
A thousand tiny hands
syncopated with my thirst

When I See You

I try to find the words to describe the body of your pleasure. A cool language of tundra or a language incandescent as water, as the ocean. All words are rooted, forests and fields overgrown with violets and acids, with physical properties of an object seeded in lead or oxygen. Let the forest grow wings and the incandescent populate the night sky! The web net fabric of your pleasure is purple pink magenta. Your veins spill over with blood and the blood is lava, rumbling into my valley. When I enter the mangle of our sexes, the deepthroated hummingbird flies.

When I see you, there are visions before me that sunflowers cannot expel, of dark roses of blood and terror pricking me with thorns. When I see you, my life is invalid with gauze, a screen of soft thickness, a desiring and bereavement found and lost. To touch, have, share you ... this is flow, or a dark corrosion of the senses, like rust building a rainbow of stone. What we give hatches the egg of an apocryphal bloom. Every moment your breathe, life stings the pale horses of my desire. Each moment the invisible arms of my love stretch across mountains. The wild hawk delivers its claw into your chest.

Ghazal of Love in Winter

Night, cold bars of gold, shivers its way
down the flushed back of day.

I am all light and tension;
the memory of rain fresh on my shoulders.

I have never seen the aurora borealis.
Our bodies are steel, sun glints from them.

Whatever is not sleeping, whatever has stored provisions
yet still hunts, is near us. Hear them?

Somewhere a hand lifts across me
a brilliant snake of emerald and orange flame.

On an island, a restless mother wakes at dawn
and carries her child to the sea.

Poet, you are sworn to secrecy.
The white thoughts are shiny fish in your hands!

IRIS

An amphibious sea snake marked with bands
of coral and umber
my hand
separates your petals
and ceremoniously
the brief transparency of your lavender
withers

Across the meadow
thick afternoon mayflies
release their mating fumes
The amulet of your scent
rides on a roan mare

Passion and dying
how the two never leave
without clasping my hand to their breasts
Near the holy bud
of the iris
their long fingers
green
wearing many rings

ST. JEROME IN HIS STUDY

After Dürer

There is a jar
buried beneath the cloister
with five words I have
kept in my pocket
all my life

solitude and wisdom
light and virtue and
a shadow of pain with thick lips
drinking from a cup

Once   in the gardens
I watched a sparrow
carry a blue silence
to the mountains

It was a rosy sorrow
I caught there
an underground rolling
of pure water
life's ever-
lasting
dahlia
sacred

How the sunlight
sweetens the room
All I own written in the very boards
what I have given away
what comes to me

The mangled flesh
of fish
in a basket
A weaving staccato
watering my soul

The almond
a taste I will never forget
brown
beautifully simple

The Bathing House

After Dürer

In the distance, the roosters crowing. The village streets
sinewy among the city's flesh and the blue skies forget-
ting why the dogs barked dropping stars from their tails
last night. You can hear cheese curdling in the buckets.
The steady heat whose organ pipes carry sweat and thirst
across the tiles and lean-tos of the village. The bodies of
men in the bathing houses. Hair skin juicy pears plucked
from trees.

For years I could lean here on this post and listen to the
flautist and the lute player marrying the spheres, carrying
harmonies with the drawstrings of their lips and fingers.
I am golden and fever, my body a gardenia whose petals
trace the navels of birds.

This herbal scent rising from my breast! A singular light,
it knows the first waters underneath the hillsides. A bright
shadow, peach and mimosa, healing the wound of the
houses as they awake at morning. The roosters bathing in
the dust and the heady men with passionate waists veined
into their eyes, wearing nothing but transparencies, leav-
ing a hush on the waters. Hands seeing birds' nests on the
terraces outside the city. A coolness I have always known
and loved.

KNIGHT, DEATH AND DEVIL

After Dürer

The lipless grin is nothing but an hourglass of fear and mule-faced devils under the horn of the moon are shrill fears I have seen and conquered. A mountain of violets trails through the rocks its final undulation of wings and Death's horses cowbells clang soundless.

I have given myself to Death many times, when my hair was black and the white dress of my youth followed the loon and the porpoise. It's lonely here, but loneliness passes, and my horse and dog march steadily onward. In the village the priest has lit his lamp by the fire of eels and there are waves around me like the voices of children.

The air is a circle of snakes! But above me, steep, a fresh bed waits. I have given myself to Death many times. Tomorrow, I'll give myself green arms above the inn and light three candles. One for each life I have named for myself, a silence anchored to a rock, honest and free, a wild unpruned tree.

GRIEFS

1

I will sit under this tree
until the rain falls in torrents
and the grass floats
in seaweed deep water
I will open my heart with a deep gash
so hungry bees
can walk between the cells of my body
I will remember a child born to poor parents
whose loved washed in shadowy green
among fruit trees
in that long ago place where
a woman entered a man's body
and beside her a bearded man
revealed his shoulders

2

Who says Grief is pale
She dresses in rainbow fire
and wears shoes of leaves and pardon
She flies up
and a blue flame showers from her face

3

My old aunt
once had a dream of me
drunk with sorrow riding down
from the mountains
with apples
plaited in my hair

The Golden Legend

If you ask me where I have been, I would have to tell you of
the journey. Of high mountains like castles of craggy ice and
a black moon whistling in the sky, a sky spun of metals. I
would tell you of strange islands green among ice on corners
of snow, wonderful birds like agate blue with crimson heads
crimson with green heads speckled with golden heads. As if
from slumber or deep hypnosis, I would rise from my chair,
placing my arms around your head and trace the shape of
your neck, the shape of your shoulders, the quiet slope of
feathers escaping from your armpits. I would describe our
first night on the islands, how, when the moon hid behind
the pines, feathers grew on us and when we bathed, they fell
off.

I would embrace you gently with a year's worth of love and
tell you how these birds drew pictures in the sand. How
their mercury music echoed on the waves! When they sang,
feathers dropped from our navels, tracing the architecture of
our bodies, and we asked ourselves the worth of this jour-
ney without a soul of snow, a birdlike soul rising out of wild
colors, embracing wind, drawing symbols of transformation.
Reading the golden legend, this is the story I might tell you,
watching orange-green orchids flying from your throat!

SHEDDING THE OLD SELF

In silence's adored and silkened embrace
I shed my body   its skin a fragrant
papershell a narcissus
I shed it again and again
under the old motherly moon
I shed it in dreaming's womb
and always it remains the same
wrinkled and smooth

Soft body of sunflowers
body of iris blue and yellow body
you taste and smell of olives
and geraniums
With the strength of stones
you settle on the earth

and I shed you
like light on a mountain
under the sea
or a robe fresh woven
falling gracefully to the ground

BESTIARY

If I should drop my robes you would see
that I am dressed in quills of diamond
and the light from the cuts are small
animals in a wood, rabbits and sparrows,
iridescent witch-doctors and damp salamanders,
blind and alert. Resilient and silent,
my skin hums with the sounds
of darkness. If you look carefully
through the vines you will see it
breathe. I am a white snail trailing
a diadem of minerals under the leaves.
I return at dawn and follow the lines
drawn by my belly in the night. The final
decomposition of a man, fear swirling near
the antennae. What kind of stranger
to himself opens the cauldron of midnight
and then denies it? What kind of spinner
of webs, like the harvester weaves in the
fields, spurns the hidden laws when the world
is light? Fear that I know, make a knot
of black steel and capture me in it. I
should brush my hair and pinch my cheeks.
I should enter the kitchen and watch
the squash boil. I should follow the dust
rolling under the table. In this way
oh self, the being of nothingness can
answer me. The rich oil of night will
cover my skin, a sheen of witness to myself,
so I might take life like a lower and lower
myself to heavens and ditches, as if my
human bark alone were the songs of the crane
and my orange beak and blue feathers
the world I live in.

THIS SMALL LIGHT

For Ron

This small light
I have coated with pollen
and brought to you
opens many doors
to a hollow place inside me
where you may come

Water rolls down your back into bright pools
The hair on your chest
is alive and singing

Come   I gather leaves
from dark places you have never been
where two mouths
signal a fire
whose roots echo across the hills

I want you to know
one thing

This small light is yours
and comes from within you

Whoever touches it
Touches its lavender and its sting

MIDWINTER FIRES

*(1990, French Broad Press;
reprinted 2012 Seven Kitchens Press)*

*It is living and ceasing to live that are imaginary solutions.
Existence is elsewhere.*
André Breton

Midwinter Fires

All branches bare
Apple persimmon acorn
chestnut hazel
The peach gone

December   the dying month
The cold sunken
giving up of ghost

By the fires your
Moon-heat wrestling
spent harvest winds

A knock

Admit them   Admit them

Three keen-faced bulls
hindquarters manly
shaggy crouching bearing
mistletoe and holly
berry

Grieve not!
The golden bough and holly sprig
greet you!

EATING THE GOD

Having been Ox
                and Shamrock
Having been Queen
                and Peasant
Having been Tern
                and Blow-fish
This strange land
takes me

Restores my strength

The land's fleshy
                        length
        Such was our custom

With jug and grain
I by thanks am given

YULE

Let's make a fire
to cure poison

We'll smolder a log
shoulder sorrows away
in brass buckets
                        of ash
        Luck will be ours

        The singing flint within us
Embers glowing
                glowing

SATURNALIA

I left the place I was accustomed to
Where the rooster
ignites and hails

                  the sun

You find me

          A goat

                with a black

beard

IN MY JACKET

                with turmeric designs
I am straw
            forsaken
      but my thighs
are fresh sea-water
full with black
             fishes

Why have you yet to
                    cast a line?

Winter Dusk

Faint heliotrope shadows
                              on the slopes
Halos of slanted light
                    slight like young
                                        goats
          Shapely gods
                    two young men
          fingering near the oaks
Nubian ears
                    long enough
          to capture the sheer
                              glory

PRINCIPLES

Electrical magnetic archonic
lucent vitric cerulean
Will-o'-the wisp
Moon dog
St. Elmo's beacon

Without these
                    roots lie callow
        Birth
                    waits in the wings

GNOSIS

Green clusters on the vine
Such a well-fruited handsome bush
                  of lush
                          sap-rising

With my forefinger
I rub the new bud

THE HOLLY

Beads
      of blue
               blood
the air transfigures
                  crimson
A crown
          of thorny
     green

The sun does not die
            The earth tapers
                  then savors
                       its shine

In the wood's gloom
            a blazing
                 evergreen

Cow-Born Dionysus

Here you are again
Friend of the winnowing heart
Back from your far journey

I will help you work the
                              lath and hoop
        to set the stars on
                an unbitter loop
        so your sacred frame
        will hang low and succulent
        like the eyes
                        of new calves

WHEN I WAS TAKEN

                                        by the eternal
                                                    Light
out of the garment that was upon me,
and taken up to a holy place whose likeness
cannot be revealed in the world,
there by means of a great blessedness I saw

Seth's mark upon you
below your left buttock
a coarse patch of hair
                    triangular
            where he touched you

The Thrice Male   The Living Milk

            A stillness
                        A silence

            Within me

◫

I am a battle-waging spear
I am a god who sets the head afire with smoke
Who knows this
                knows me

POEMS FROM THE FOUNTAIN

(1992, North Carolina Wesleyan College Press)

Of the pursuit of beauty, and the husk that remains.
Williams Carlos Williams

*Those who are awake have a common world, but those
who sleep turn aside, each into his own particular world.*
Heraclitus

*Sell your cleverness and buy bewilderment.
Cleverness is mere opinion, bewilderment is intuition.*
Jalaluddin Rumi

The weariness of the heart is the root of an unbelievable courage.
Frantz Fanon

THE SONG

There is a song inside me
It is white and bright
like a boat at its moorings
It is black and sad
and will not break
I will not give it to the Puritans

There is a song inside me
What a color it has
I have its color
Violet violet
Black and sad
How witchly I will sing it

THE SPELL

To see my Gods
                    to charm
                    their nudity
with
a word
            I assume
                    a buck's
                    sleek neck
steal
        a quail's
        small mouth

THERE

Let the fog
awakening us each day be
a start.
and the stars
in their cleverness
please you.

Stones
bound together by moss
and years are
no more clever, nor
the stars, than your
steadfastness.

Such is the foolishness
of men
who would not know
love,
they would turn
deaf

to the challenge.
As for me,
I did not ask to
enter the needle's
eye.
The painted turtle

in the long light
of ponds
can go through.
But not me, I said.
and yet,
I find myself

there.

COMPARISONS

He turned
slightly
askew

At profile
an Incan god
a golden brown
boy

The birds
on this mountain
are sleek and
sly

Some are blue
Some chew the leaf
Some do not

ANTINOUS IN EGYPT

> *I myself felt a kind of terrible joy at the thought that that death*
> *was a gift. But I was the only one to measure how much bitter*
> *fermentation there is at the bottom of all sweetness, or what*
> *degree of despair is hidden under abnegation, what hatred is*
> *mingled with love.*
>
> Marguerite Yourcenar, *Memoirs of Hadrian*

Falcon. You were not enough.
Protection is a harsh device.
Comes only with the proper tools,
the appropriate sacrifice. You knew
that as well as I.

You served me well. At the end your
hooded sleepy face never betrayed
the wilderness in your blood. The hungry
talons: so like myself in my impetuous love.
Clutching for him took the uncanny
form of physical drowning in a spiritual glove.

All gives way. All lights extinguish.
White roses curl five petals
under Venus's star. My skin oozes
in honeyed ointment. No struggle
in the Nile. No pain. Just litany
and drowsy darkness claiming me.

Hadrian, my master. I am your Genius
speaking to you from the grave.
Know this enchantment binds!
I am your falcon, will follow
every arrow. No spear can harm me.
When the hunted falls, they will
be my prey.

A youthful oddity I am! So few sense
Death's power. The sheer curtain
keeping us from it. The blaze, oh,
the blaze! Earthly passions pale before it.

The priests ignite their incense, murmuring
their prayers—supplications to the multitudinous
flower of the spheres. Red poppies flash
faces at the gate—black throats groaning.

Falcon. You were not enough.
Together we had to go, swelling
the blood-bloom sinew in his chest.

Sebastian At Seige

Mother, the air is a thief.
It steals salt from the body, loosens
the Will, until it splays out, liquid.
I sit straight up in bed, naked,
looking in the mirror. This, my body,
which I consume. The tendons
and frets on which it hangs.
Hating it once, it is now so beautiful, dying
in its time. Learning how to learn, to whistle
with the starlings, names a tender absolution.
In this Byzantine chamber, the air
makes a fist. An angel
bursting through the chalice of the flesh.
In these catacombs I perfect my sweat.

LEAVE-TAKING

The summons comes with the rising of the quails
you rise from the bed
pulling your fatigued pants up to your hips
The sad gourds beating together in the fields
The dead antelope carried by its feet
stops at our hut
her tender legs the goodbye of your kiss
Their shrouded flock of bone
a black mama's lips
smoothing her child's dark snake hair
When you go
your hips carry your spear through cornflower fields
Whatever I remember
is a place without birds
Whatever I remember
you come back
your beard's shadow an army of pale deer
your heart thumping in your hands
The way your lay there in the morning
the straw sensed your going
Whatever I remember
the dark umbrella of your eyes

THE MARRIAGE OF HEAVEN AND HELL

Pandora, the box smokes. No common form
mentioned by its shape.
I cannot shift my eye far from its glare.
I sense neither sound nor glimpses of desired hue.
Black the brilliant shadows sleek.
Before night falls nothing will quiet me.
Devils. I break from you my private trembling.
When I walk my shadow I will attach to me.
No formless box opens to clamp shut
unless the shutting figures me its Light-giver.
I illuminate and turn Spirit
upon itself. A healed wing.
So, I stand suddenly embracing you.
Where swarm bees imperishable.
From all blackness I gather myself.

A Valentine Metaphysic: A Song

In the dim light
smooth and

beautiful, moving
evenly

without warning or
change,

the fountain.

When you become perfect in
that place,

still yourself.
It is hard, and hot.

and, by virtue
of the pattern in you,

agile.

The Prodigal

Lost in the forest.
In the distance, clay
chimeras of towns.
Four paths and only
two feet, two hands.
At one end the hearth
I often tend.
Moon, come out,
show me the way.
Sumac, point
the right direction.
Or I shall lie down
to sleep among stones
and beetles. Tell me
morning is not so far.
Fear is my brother,
but teach me
I am mother
to my destination.

The Artist

I am not
          the moment's daughter
The sparking
               flint
               does not finish my fire
I begin
          and spread
by slow cunning
An alloy dense and rare

Mother once told me
          a shirt
                    hastily made
                    wears hastily
                    thin

Well
          my skillful rope
          never breaks

THE GIFT: A SONG

You who come from the Answerer
let it be known the wheel in the sky burns for you
and I in my clipped wings
am the child you lost in the desert
While I was gone
my feet unblessed walked
and now
the gentleness of crows
grace is upon them
Where I have come to
the fire in the hearth exits from stones
every small thing listens with new eyes
the house's dark corners notice the light
sorrow sits nowhere

FRIENDS

No formality between
friends, only
the brown,
blue, hazel-eyed beauties
in men

Will be
as
the sun
risen above the trees
risen for the bees
in their honeyed
dances

There be bees
in the sunshine
bees in the dirt
Flying in and out
buzzing and
                    centrifuging

Honey swells the ground
when you dig
                    there

On your knees
enveloped by smoke

BEAUTY AND THE BEAST

Beauty
    said the Beast

Please
    let's have a little

      peace
           some quiet between us
          a little arrogance
               perhaps

    too.
        Something sweet
    a little
        melon
    and a good time.

I'm
    not so bad

am I?

I can move you

        if you let me

try.

Hadrian from His Villa, Alone

Colder. Rarer perhaps,
than the storm.
Wait for me where
the creeping moss grows.
I know you will find
something to think about.
Listen, it's hard enough
to send messages by bird.
I have to send these
shorn and braided
by bottle. Goodnight, love.
I'll write again when
the rain ceases.

No One Else Will Do

With a nod to Gertrude Stein

I love my love with a b
because the bee stings but smells of
flowers

I love my love for trees
stand up and walk beside him
I see men as trees, walking

I love my love for a p
The prince provokes him when
the dew rises

I love my love with this and all
the other

I love him with an a
The Word created it

I love him with a zero because
I am

I love him suddenly and coarse
He should
know it

I love him with a pheasant
because Ishmael stood
the storm

Oak, cedar, birch
I love my love

Creek, rock, moss and
I do

Pear, apple, grape
He's mine

I love my love with an o
There is no other

I love my love with my cats
that I do

I do I do and here
he is a-coming

I love my love with a j
Here I join
him

A COMMON FLOWER

The chrysanthemum is
not so pink
nor so dark
as royal badges,
formal and obtuse.

Its pinkness
terrifies
as when a lamp
illuminates your palm

and a yellow glow
vibrates
through the center—
a greenness in that.

The eye
germinates in the green
honeycomb
swirling middle.

You must
bring sorrow into
clearer focus
before it.

In any house—
in this one—
shadows are not
fearsome,

but the privilege of light,
constantly visible,
where beauty
lies with

its pink
heart
severed and
slowly drowning
is.

MINOTAUR

Hic quem creticus edit Dedalus est Laberinthus
de quo nullus vadere quivit qui fuit intus
ni Theseus gratis Adriane stamine iutus

This is the labyrinth which the Cretan Daedalus built, out of which
nobody can find his way except Theseus, nor could he have done it
unless he had been helped by Ariadne's thread, for love.
    From the cathedral at Lucca, on the church porch,
    translated by Guy Davenport

    For Anais Nin

1

Deep the well
                    Deep also its darkness
winding out
                    and in
the deep
            opalescence
                                        lit
from the twilight bridge
spun between

2

Love
            the first cause
I sing of
            the bull
            in druidic white
            frothy white   as veils
            in Pasiphae's
            dream chambers were white
            bells

3

                    Of flowering

                                  narcissus
I sing

of
        he who of this earth(sea)
        wrestled the bull
        among mothwings'
                  glitter of comings
                              and goings

4

From night
        a breast-plummeting bird

That love
        may make martyrs of us
        in the heart's quartered house
        I build a labyrinth
        peopled by the half-bull

5

In this city
        likenesses of fire
        of fire

        we, the seduced

        given

SAPPHO NOW

Sappho now, and other
times Catullus.
Occasionally a prowling Celtic medium.
Always the dark worm in the words.
Always, pungent chrysanthemum.

ARS POETICA: THE QUEEN

In collaboration with my others
I build this hive. As I am
Goddess, this, then, is my cathedral.
Built of wax and lives. Of light
and honey.
It grows around me.

My first sensation
was of yellow: a hum
forcing my skin to see.
Since then I have sung
the praises of this operation.

When You Stop to Rest

the swallows
in you
remain
in you

SUBMERGENCES

(1997, Off the Cuff Books;
reprinted in Madder Love 2008)

A writer starts out to describe a kingdom of castles and horses,
but ends tracing the lines of his own face.
Jorge Luis Borges

I am obscure as feeling is.
Pierre Reverdy

To enter. The heart must shatter.

◻

It all began empty snow-white black velvet: an assault on the dark edges. Crickets howled at the house. The house lay secret, wanton. A gross bile echoed in the rooms. Rooms of toys rooms of gingham rooms plastered with a child singing in the night his arms flung out the window into a southern inflated summer of crepe myrtle and violets. Wine plum cerise starlight flickered on my tiny feet shuffling to the window. A tiny narrow garden a smoky garden a frightened and frightening garden shivering in its horrible aspect of sweet ambassadors hidden among flowers. and a voice whispered to me in the darkness, to the child of age the child of woe whistling in the mirror the darkeyed child the secret child the child alone the childman leaning out the window:

Let your hair barely bronzed naked tattooed in scarlet the marks where the act lives in joy, dies with better hope.

I knew, then, the being inside this ribbon of flesh. I knew the ribbon stroking the darkness.

◻

Rims of scarlet. Gold. Olive leaves. Rims of thickness descending on arcs of ruby. *Mica. Fluorspar. Tourmaline.* Silver white purple loose blackness. The mirage.

I am a child, watching words form in my mouth which then fall clumsily to the floor—remarkable, magical communion with godliness. I am responsible towards these words. Taking us somewhere we have not been. Defining the world, the known.

Beautiful beautiful life with what has been and has not been me asking to become part of something it has not seen and seeing it part of me within it part asking to understand and understanding again its silverness its part which shines and the dull the whole beneath the inside and lightning lightning no not fleece but unbearable seeing which knows O knows so seeing inside beautiful life beautiful life asking of nothing asking.

The thing which is beauty. Is itself. Broken. Light under a cornice. In a wayward room. Unvisited.

Here are the young. They beat the white hairs on our chests until we cry to love them. Ravenously, I pluck hairs stuttering at the fall of some most holy penitents.

◳

Always water. Always loose weeping because we dare not blame ourselves.

◳

You will say you remember me on that last day when frozen we stutter through ice. You will say motion is between us, that years of speaking to and for each other has its boundaries, has a word or meaning or symbol discernible in the future beyond our pain or invisible hatred of departure and that we are its captive. But I have the odor of your lips next to my eyes. I cast off the weight of poison the dart your odor spins into my heart. The ice forces my hands into an arch, a yogic tempo of pleasure shooting through them. I forget odors and figures I forget the seething power of hatred the seething power of blueblack wounds and the rush of blood to the temples. Our journeys, perilous. My vapors mix with the infinite.

◳

Outside the moon eats at white shadows
with its mirror

Night's green glare
simmers in the woods
The sleepers gone

Wild lilies stare at the stars
Three in the morning
the fire trains lions in a circle of weeds
The lions hearts of red hawks without eyes

The lilies weightless
dragging their carcasses behind them

The sleepers rustle in coat sleeves

Now the moon shudders
at its face in the mirror
nudging the fire
As lions swoop among the pines
sleepers sweep the ashes
mocking its restlessness

And the Shadow enters me. Enters the snapdragon path in the
center of my chest, the bronze being murmuring in my stom-
ach, captivated by release, captivated by the body of pain. I
remember now the vast sun unpeels its skin each winter—a
lizard. The golden chiefs give feathers of blue to hide their
magic in ... women of citrus gather blossoms the moon gives
them soaking the petals for oils. The sleek triumph of a man's
body insistent all-owning transparent tiger-lilies lasting only
an hour in the jar. Married in water divorced by it shimmer-
ing evaporate, my skin moults in the jar, leaving a residue
of fragrance and blood, residue of light boiling in the bowl.
Death strides through my belly, awakening the mum-odor of
silence, a vast unbreakable silence pure as granite thick as
noon snow. As I turn, a face lifts its fisheyes from the snow.

Quietly the white settles on my shoulder. Alone with the moon, my ointments bleed into the streets, leaning forever against the dragonwings of the sun.

The heart palpitates under the windows. Pane after pane. Reflecting bubbles in the glass.

In clear domes, the way light cowers in the corners. Waiting to be discovered.

We brood heat in a glacier. The glacier descends in perfect rhythm as I deny its closeness. But the cold belt soothes, chipping away at the green carousel: my memory of the future. I look graciously forward, aware that you have touched me. The tiny cilia of doubt sipping at ice: fear of the unknowable blank margins of space where I forfeit control to the inner world. I give in. The glacier swelters, crushing my imagined freedom. The inner voice. The unknown.

A white line on a wharf. Decade after decade of facing the firing. Dull gulls, mink cups from which we drink words. Reckless and starving, leaving exhilaration behind with monotony. Afraid to believe.

■

We hurtle toward oblivion. Holding ourselves back but
crazy with the desire to unite with it. What is the un-
known?

■

Against your hand
my body twists a flower
struggling to blossom
Pollen sweating through the stamens

We clamor   now   at the center
of the sun
My waist rising out of a pit
churning you wet

I gasp   bleed minerals
feeding the root
Its exotic urge
separating sweetflesh
from the spirit
while I rage
at transient intensity
flinging the hole of the body
into space

This fever I know
unlocks gold
A mystery stone
A potion
seen in dreams

Charting the course
we might take with love's body
my waist
held in your hands
Slipping wetness from vials
eroding the foundations of your heart

Thrown weeds caught between my legs. Pollen devouring the naked man running over pebbles his earrings his ears black with unspoken words unheard themes. Insects eating at the semen's gore. I draw three circles round the lizard. His tongue a rock. Twists of the lizard's tail point towards the stars. I buckle into sleep.

The lapse of time between the initial glance and the final expected moment of confrontation seems like ages. Time, when one is hesitant, when one cares deeply and awaits much, drags—a web of spidery silk, snagging every effort to move, to complete the journey from one room to the next. The rose grows thorns and buds. The vine gathers its mesh. The web: embracing a shiny ebb-quiet rowing towards love—mixed blossoms with fragrance impacted so strong I feel no guilt, no hesitancy to complete the collision. Interstices of the dream.

The wind knows no one tonight
but we
The sleepers thick under
the stars
We have no arms nor legs
nor torsos
No ground
nor seed

We who have not the urge
have not the sense
We who have
shiver in quintessence

The kind murder of renunciation. A velvet bomb exploding
hate's retina. I learn to love, learning to hate. Hate rises out
of the body, flagellating the senses, penetrating layers of my-
self. Testing my strength. The quick sleeve of guilt stifling
efforts to move and be. Love releases guilt. Releases hate.
Trial by fire and the whistle.

Using the body as a tool to realize
itself
in all its infirmities

bloodpassing
through watery soap
Using the sweatboiled rim of skin
hung in an arc
on a band of light
Crazy light of fabulous fingers
in the core

Where are your hands that have touched? Where the soul in
your eyes? Hair down deep—fish in gull wings singing. You
know the fairy tale. You, the hands that bleat in darkness.
The root. Wild refreshing billow of hands. Pillow of hands.
My pillow: a nail hammered in red parachutes of tourmaline.
Your hands pigeons in my back. Arched holy saints of fishes.
Hands in their blue suits of love fishing out whales humming
in alabaster.

I come before noon with wind anchoring my stomach. Wool
banging shutterless against dawn and your hands. I am the
black sparrow you knew. The cautious lover tucked under
your brow. The beaten paradise. I cannot see, needing your
hands trumpets of wine and smoke chattering my tongue.
My waist. My infinity in your hands.

◻

If I dismantle the cragginess of lips—lamps without oil. If I
lay both sides of a coin on the groin of words—a bitter green
like a wild form. If I persuade the sickness to come out—
morning will rise with the hooves of angels on the streets.

◻

Aphrodite bore me from the waves
neither son nor daughter I am
the mixed bloom of contradictory
elements fused into a sonata
the subtleties *bloodstone agate*
ruby quartz plows under the swamp
thickets grow jailcells cages
blacker than an eclipse of stone
Manwoman I bring forth my lizard
repeating the endless series of
circles the lizard leaps into
my mouth and escapes carrying
my voice to the

           wind
           rain
           sun

◻

He gives me fruit. Lemons tangerines bananas melons. His
wings spattered with moonlight. Taking me inside his stom-

ach full of juices: birdsong in a storm of flutes. *Peacock blue magenta fuchsia limegreen salmon black.*

The fruit is good.

Your eyes: filters of smoke deepening thickly the ominous chaos of this illusion. I ask myself, why so fearful? Chaos......confusion. Muddled in my own sensitivity. The room softens—each object at once harsh and threatening—transforms. I see you, your eyes sweeping away falling into the chorus of love.

We travel in a panther's stomach. Riding for days passing through villages farms forests saints on their way to Hell with thick beards of ivy-tangled words floating between their mouths matted with holiness. A moth trapped inside. I try desperately to shake it through the layers of silk. It flutters and dies while its new wings glisten with coats of lacquer and slobber minutes ago mummified in its cocoon waiting for its gauzy wings to shine melt under the sun's rays. This moth trapped inside the panther

> dead
> for
> lack of sun
> lack of air.

> The moth
> smothered in love.

His penis
flower
of flowers

      Indigo
      cotton
      ears of corn

      morning glories
      sunflowers
      the Ivory Coast

The men paint themselves with rushes
to attract the wind
each layer of
pink
yellow
burgundy
indigo

      a net painted with rain

His penis

a flower blooming in
dark mirrors
Yellowred
its mothy odor rises inside
a frosted circle

Geraniums nasturtiums grape-ivy
pour from its tip

The men grease themselves
with berries
turning their skin
purple and black

Gumming
their hairy thighs with
hashish and opium

The panther falters at the garden pool. Goldfish reflected in his eyes dart out then in panging with fear. I want to touch him. I want to heal wounds. I see only my own crystal, my own shattering against the torrent of the whirl-pool. Down down I am pulled into the mass of weeds. I throw up my hands and grasp the rushes the cattails. The panther's sleek torso trembles milkweed in a snow storm. I forget myself give the goldfish sunshine water algae fruit refusing to die grasping life with fertile hands pushing into the deep well of love. The panther slits me from neck to navel and begins to chewspit chewspit necklaces of pearl into my groin. I swell in water lifting my eyes to the wind the rushes. *Indigo purple burgundy.* I touch his eyes.

Beads collected in a pool
I come like orchids in a field
White mahogany
my garnet skin stacked beside the fire
Stripped
I envy nothing but a wild rain of stars
upon the palm of space

You tell the story of your emotions. I do not know you, you say. I cannot know you. The you I see is not the you which is you. The you which you have known for your lifetime. The you I see is the you of Now. What is your Now, is yourself, transforming. We live in a mirror. I see your reflection in my own. Never ourselves but what we see in each other. The mirror's white teeth creating images of hand-to-hand....the laid-back motion of our bodies.

If whiskers grow straight on the mountains
when the tremors kiss
I will know you

■

Men surround me with tongues of fire. They shout garbled idioms into the air. Daisies! As the tension builds, skyscrapers exPLODE! Farms exPLODE! Sexes EXplode! Nothing is the same. I finger a crimson lute, all eyes upon me. I faint, singing to *Hermaphroditus Uroboros Gorgon Quetzalcoatl Tiamat.*

■

We set ourselves to task. Four of us form a square, an easily constructed, easily destroyed, grouping of men. Fragile. Mummified in foil. Reflecting the burns.

■

Inside the square we draw intersecting lines of diagonals. Some men enter the box and surround it. Extending the diagonals, they create two large triangles that lessen the descent of water. Fanning of flames. We appear as two wings of a kite balanced, beautiful infinitely unstable. Eager to change in wind.

Each man enclosed in the womb. The furnace quiet.

One man
narrower through the thighs
Purple
spread over it all

The leafy heads of
Emerald-eyed
blackberry bushes
Molten rock
to the level of the trees

Inside was even more

We have soldiers who go
to save a tiny fish:
the shape, musky hailstones
beneath the earth's crust

Lichens grow on infants
All emotion
wounded
from zero to sixty in an elegant maroon
of space into a
mouth and dropped away as if dead

The physical body
you enter
silver-backed
staccato

Water: a hand of liquid beauty. Silk-wrapped, mummified
in foil, the bodies eat at each other. I fear the light which
smothers dark, carrying each layer of words deeper into the
thrust my wound lays open. Water eats at fire. Fire eats at
sky. Sky trembles and screams crumbling toy blocks into
liquid sediment.

When I awake, I discover a small star-shaped tattoo on my
left cheek. Barely perceptible from my olive skin, it vibrates
against my seeing it. One moment it is there, the next it
seems only a slight flaw in the skin.

By afternoon, it becomes bright scarlet. By nightfall, a deep
thick magenta. I feel no pain, but some transformation over-
comes me.

When from the corona
soft
you pour your dire flame
Eruption
a mountainous geography
enters my mouth
We
the obscured elements
compose a spiralling
of flesh
seven times

the world's length and breath

Into the abrupt sentence
gasp
and call from the Above
the soul-creature
Corona
At our green roots
bowls
shiny filmy tendrils
ooze out their glass
to attraction's poles now stretch
their dun hairs
by love possessed

Mitered and uncorrupt

I
the plucked
damson
your terrible embrace exposes

Name me One

                    an exile from the body-prison
        into soul-stuff strung

Singing a lark
caught in a deep well
throttled heaping wind
through pipes of water
piercing barriers of stone
out into the sunlit world

        I cry

When the day grows dark, I sift slowly through galaxies and nebulas.
Unbound my earth. A golden bar upon which I lean.

AFTERWORD

The altar...is anywhere you kneel. Camille Paglia

This piece, written over forty years ago, reflects the early impact, the deliriously heady influence, of Rimbaud, the Symbolists, Anais Nin, Edith Sitwell, shattering radical feminist works by Monique Wittig [*Les Guérillères* and *The Lesbian Body*] and, particularly, French Surrealism, had on my aesthetic [before I came to know Spanish Surrealism, which too left its mark on me.] To look back from the oftentimes minimalist, Objectivist (and essentially American), spare simplicities I move in now, is to remember Mies van der Rohe's "Less is more." Recalling also that opposites bear each other's seeds—to be over-elaborate, unconscious, abstracted, unrestrained, and ecstatic, is also to be ecstatic, simple, conscious, concrete, and restrained. In both, the silence of all silences can be heard. If one can listen. To many, *Submergences* may seem nonsensical, downright self-conscious, and imprecise. To me, written under Surrealism's banner using automatic writing (with very little revision now as we go to press), I see the gates of Heaven and Hell thrown open, and the poet's subconscious as a beacon from another reality. The unfolding youthful love relationship narrated in *Submergence*s hurled me into a Melvillian "Encantada"—a bleakness, a romance, a strangeness, a wild beauty. In these words already throbs the longing for the Divine which stills propels my writing, the struggle to unite the Body and the Spirit into One Knowledge, One Transfiguration. Although pure Surrealism is not a mode in which I now write, it modulates my sensitivities still, even as I speak.

POEMS FROM
VISIONS OF DAME KIND

(1995, The Jargon Society)

In the Vision of Dame Kind distinctions between the beautiful and the ugly, the serviceable and the unserviceable, vanish. So long as the vision lasts the self is "noughted," for its attention is completely absorbed in what it contemplates; it makes no judgments and desires nothing, except to continue in communion...In some cases the subject speaks of this sense of communion as if he were himself in every object, and they in him.
W. H. Auden

The Death

For Christian Moon

1

At field's edge sumac
broods
its foul September torch.

Its blood berries singe the night.
Maroon and lovely.

2

The marguerites have taken over
the town garden. The golden
marguerites. Rampant, pungent.

3

From the tiny worms in my gnawed
heart, I welcome silence.
The heavy pollen
of a face
crossing the hill.

Lanky. Orange.

Oisin*

Four horses
manes afire,
stamping
in a mist—

cyclamen and chestnut.

Their chests heave
astonishing the bracken.

*I am a shaking tree,
my leaves,
gone
from me*
roaming the raw
highlands
and ravines.

*Oisin's Laments from Lady Gregory's Gods and Fighting Men

COCKSCOMB

A rooster crows.

The flower god's
anxious
with blossom.

I lower my head
to yours,
praising
the bittersweet
burdens
of men.

THE BAMBOO THICKET

For D.H. Lawrence

You have only to look
to hear

boys walking through you
The thwack thwack

of sticks
and stones

Live Oaks

I turn from the drowned
shaking my

wet beard
into

your isolated grove.

JEWELWEED

Turning the woodland path
Pale-touch-me-not
at creek's edge.

At edge,
impatient,
don't touch me.

STONECROP

For Walt Whitman

I will not
lead

the muddy cows of
despair

to the rocks.
But mix

with pliant juices
the clear, bold

sun
light

of this pasture.

PASTORAL

I should have some seedlings
tomorrow
some columbine fit for a king's
chamber—
the clamoring stream side
by the garden
where we'll lie

Not enough for cutting now but
come Spring
all swell and bell will
break loose

SPANISH MOSS

over trees.
         Old beards
hung
    to dry.

These days
      we have lived
in each other's
        shadows.

How easy
      to confuse
the sleek
triumph of
     a man's body.

My Great-Great-Grandmother Arrives in the New World

This piedmont field
full of cornflowers

How many unlived
threads will I hold on to

My whole life-blood means
departure

CANZONE

Rosemary

              Fireflies

      Bees

I who love many
have always loved

thee

TRITOMA

Flame flower
Maleness drawn from shadows
Grief is your mother
Chanticleer of the flowers

LADYSLIPPER

Dark orchid
the nightgown of your body
unfolds
Rain comes down
with black tresses
around
me

TULIP TREE

This tulip thrown down from a heaven of green stars
Six petals two-thirds green
Orange bargello before the yellow
The phallic flame

Fading too fast for human hands
Incan   Worn on the breast
A song sung out loud to oneself
in a dark room

Mosquitos beat against the screens
and still they fall

MADRIGAL

I will love you with
hands of gentians
so the warmth of your skin
will be the warmth of
apples ripened
The red of
summer clover

The Question

The persimmon tree
heavy now
with dusty fruit.

Which
is sweeter?
That going? Or
that gone?

FIGS

1

Seven figs and no one to eat them?
Seven figs for Seven Wisdoms.
Some for breakfast, some for dinner.
Who will split them?
Serve them cold, or lay them
in the sun.

2

These crouch on table
rumps upturned
round as the arrow is not
but as the arrow aimed at
heart's center.

THE PARABLE OF KINGS

With first warmth
the blackberry
puts out its lime-colored
leaves.

Last year
Lord Dog and I
painted our lips, pawing
black-green arches for
red-black elegances.

King Jonathan said,
Men of Shechem, die
the death of shunned
ungrateful wretches
who know not
the dignified bramble,
King of Trees, honored
for its humility.

Sweet Fennel

Ah, here in the
tall grasses
Foeniculum umbels
of green and yellow.

Rubbing my bare chest
with sweetness and
soft fern,
the tongue swooning.
Profound
unisons.

HELLEBORE

With arms of
green and rosy blossoms
my blameless love
comes.

Blessed by cows and
sorcerer's spittle,
I pass
though the air, dark,
leaf-shining,
invisible.

FINDINGS

I took the apple
from where it fell
and went down
under the grass
under the pasture's last
wave of
goldenrod light
where the mole's
inner sanctum lies
where the apple seed
is a bead of sweat
in the cool earth.

I found there:
the sun and the
third thing.

The Gnats

Stroked by the presence of gnats
I'm sitting in the sun
animal
        naked

POEMS FROM GOSPEL EARTH

(2010, Skysill Press)

*He who has seen everything empty itself is close to
knowing what everything is filled with.*
Antonio Porchia

To all those suffering, involuntarily, from their imaginations.
Henri Michaux

ILLUMINATIONS

What use is prose when what we are speaking of is the poem? I take up pen finding wide silences that do not ache to be filled. Spaces between things and thoughts seek me out. Shadows fill my poems. In that illumination is the Word. I seek the Beloved—the pearl ribbons He leaves behind. I listen for silent bells. I smell sweet flowers near the intelligent lowly ground. I look in the last place we would not think to—in the discarded shattered world. Someone asked Rumi that if he, indeed, really believed in silence, then why did he talk, sing, and dance so much. He replied, "The radiant one inside me never speaks."

As I went to sleep last night after beseeching whatever help I could—I was much distressed —I was hit by something on my forehead—not light, not the feeling of a real fist—but a distinct sensation of force colliding with skin—a sheath of protection dropping over me. It had no emotional content—very plain and simple—as if a door or window had closed, or a curtain been quietly drawn.

PARADISO

I go where
feathers blow

World

In the Mimosa Tree

Words came to me and oh they smelled peach but shaggy

HEADGAME

Coarse silk rubbing my brow
Furrows and wind tunnels
The door shuts twice

Lovers' Wisdom

Panting in grass beneath high air sun

SACRED MARRIAGE

Swaggering kisses along needled forehead terraces

Baptism

Red ash rains
Your breath:
                    articulate

When light descends give
sorrow a tender
weeping a hair

STRANGER IN A STRANGE LAND

Bees sense crowshadow across dry pavement

I am pilgrim on this vegetable earth

WINTER IS THE WORLD,
SUMMER THE OTHER REALM*

Dirt dauber's black iridescence drinking from cat water bowl
Does love's pain diminish or heighten this?

*Gnostic *Gospel of Philip*

COMMENTARY ON *DUENDE*

I thank you for
this immense
sulfurous melancholy

Despite the sirocco
the miracle happens

So the High Pasture

tenders them
tearing their scent
across the wide hill
sky bending down
to meet them

What is here
What bleating bell beneath
mountain's green sun
What hoof print writing
horns arched
locked in rhythm

Secret Gospel

The other world lord
with his rain buckets splashing
with his heart coming a wind
with his translucent looks ravishing
with his copper-ring circling his head
with one river rising
with one river emptying

He keeps turning round the certain mountains
Bringing me back
My seaweed skirt shivering emerald
So I can say the unsayable

To live is to sleep
Awakening the first longing
at dream's gate

Inner Light

I have seen it when I remember to forget to look
when I remember it is there with my back turned my heart
towards it surf bringing up tarnished impossible boats
through brackish waters and countless smooth pure sands

RESURRECTION

What late fire-dragons
fume from my body
What purples
What frosts

The night tastes bitter

Dawn's
moss on my tongue

Beauty

HELIOS GOSPEL

Standing naked in the sun I
am not like a wolf because

I am the sun

Foggy Mountain Sutra

Black shadows in the room outdoor fog at bay

Fog drops shadow drops transparence window

In limitless fog branches silhouetted against gray dawn
Who are you now

Beyond thick mist sky beyond thick mist sun
Who knows where light sleeps

Close your eyes clock ticking
Open them clock ticking still

Fog night's gray feathers down lifted
Fog dawn's gray feathers at rest

Lift fog from gray-black beech limbs find black-gray fog

See me in the green by fog world's ocean
Illusion doesn't want me fog needs me

A fog hat on the fern fronds a frog plop on the frog pond

Marl grass blanket for winter's beetles no birds fly

Halfway up slope spring burbles into fog morning
Not only water not only sound

I hunger for all I don't see
What sees me hungers more
World without foggy end

Anxious to waken anxious to go out
What gray bones dance me to my grave

Mountain pillows to rest fog cushions in dream's land

Why keep dreaming loss fog filters eye iris
Fog thickens blood love stiffens love

Still night lingers fog holds sun in its cup
Waiting for the right moment now

Lilac Days in the Lot Valley, France

magpies battling on tile roof below the windows
sun setting between steel clouds lilacs blooming

wake up! mind hears bird's green breath responds
wake up! birds hear mind's lilac breath respond

I realize
often unseen
we burst into starry flames
perhaps a nettle
green and less intensely blue
A high entrance
A reassuring yellow
Singing nostalgic romances

and when it is well
add honey or cooked grape
hunks of bread
and wine then
a full moon rise

Men of Toulouse

What love to be made with such sunshine in the body

Drought

Never mind the moonlight liquid on my eye garden
Divine light never ceases

Aurelius Says

Let the deity within you be the guardian of a living being
Red on the black gum leaves
Ants crawling on my neck skin tingling
Goldenrod's green gold river wind

Humility nourishes everything
Do good so you would soothe
Your face should always be shining

The Visitation: Moth

No flame to explain me

And Yet

I am alone
understanding the world
shuffles great grievances

and yet

and yet

WHAT IS THE SOUND

of
   before I was born
of
   before I was dead

of
   the broken-winged bird

MINOTAUR EXPOSED

For John Menapace

> *We shall not cease from exploration*
> *and the end of all our exploring*
> *Will be to arrive where we started*
> *and know the place for the first time*
> T. S. Eliot

Think often of my eyes:
Through one forged of
steel and glass
I view the world

Eye awakens:
Not the water, but
*a patterned energy made visible**
by it:

Silence
music reaches for:

Still point where
notes gather pattern
path meets pathway

If there were a place
I could enter
I would enter it finding
the door in the wall the wall itself
This side that side

vanishes
Endlessly here endlessly not

A door opens:
Neither somewhere nor nowhere
On the other side either
something or nothing

Close your eyes you
hear it

Open them

Is it gone?

I shape wood into mist
I make grasses into water
I grow my hair long
and white

The eye looking straight on hears
the zigzag electric
in the upright thing

There! A crack
in the wall
A moment's verdant skin
dense with ceremony and resemblances

Green will out

I leave my chambered room
Yet another nautilus summons me
Death's river beyond the courageous door
Living door beyond the tranquil world

Setting forth even lazy boats startle in anticipation

Receive me O compassionate
entrances and exits!

O world made contradictory and real
by time, men, and wander arriving!

I knew you even before my eye
I knew you before the first leap scarred my heart
When love thundered through the corridors
and brutality relinquished me

A Holiness in the wor(l)d
Enter into its courts with praise

*Hugh Kenner

MY BIRTH/DAY

I came to wildblossopening
in womb's April

Possession Sutra

I knock at
the door

No one answers

I knock at the door
again

No one comes

No one comes
I ask
Who are you

I am no one
Who are you

Then
No body

THE GREEN MAN'S MAN

The mind, that ocean where each kind
Does straight its own resemblance find;
Yet it creates, transcending these,
Far other worlds, and other seas,
Annihilating all that's made
To a green thought in a green shade.
    Andrew Marvell

Green, I want you green.
Green wind. Green branches.
    Federico Garcia Lorca

For a long time I
stand at the oak's foot
asking it

What can you tell me of
time   weather

Its heartbeat doesn't stop
It moves ahead in
its rooted place
swaying its canopy in the wind

Dark wind   Bright wind
It never says a word
It just keeps talking

In order to make sense
of the ground
I build an earthen hill and sit upon it

The ants welcome me as their brother
Bees radiate out in golden circuits
while above the oaks' light-hungry leaves
spread wide   The clouds
call me
                        changing their forms

Each day I visit my mound
till one day the rains come
Then I float
happy and wet
among the tadpoles' delight
the moccasins' white-mouthed praise

�«»

I ask the wind to carry me
and it does
                        Opening my catkins
I make it rain yellow
I make sunshine into powder

�«»

I open Nature's book
finding:
The more I know
The less I know

Finding under the oak:
"majesty in a creeping snail"
"deliberation"   "seriousness"
"shyness and yet
what absolute trust"
"the deeply slumbering spirit within"*

Once when the hurricane slammed the oak
to the ground
I walked stunned within its branches
elaborate with mistletoe

Girth sacrificed to its friend wind
Dignified even then

Oak:
"A garden and country"**
Father to perpetual fire
Channel of the gods and goddesses
Opening heaven's crack
Last leaf never falling

I, in my green shirt,
put on my broad antlers
sure-footed, Druidic, lichen-dressed

A wizened-woodman

To entice the eye
into the mysteries of time and weather
I sprout leaves

◙

The oak my father

Twig in winter
Bud in spring
Leaf in summer
Acorn in autumn

◙

All that I am:

A woodpecker at dusk and dawn
on the white oak trunk

A cardinal flower at field's edge reading cloud
                                        shadows

The cardinal points—every direction a good and
                                        purposeful one

Every oak an axis through earth's center

◙

Ah, the lacewing's found the horn-of-plenty at
                                        the oak's foot

◙

Sometimes I think there are two of me
for my arms are so big I embrace so much
It just doesn't seem that I can be just one

But then One is what I am and
like being
as all the oaks are One Oak
as all rivers roar into One

I sit at my table counting
the times an acorn hit me
on the head
or the times I looked up straight
up into glinty leaf frissons
when the sun's brevity broke
through the multitude and
I, too, looked down at myself
"Green thought in a green shade"

The blue jay quarrelsome as
he is
                    has style

For this the oak befriended him
Together they made a forest
one
              acorn
              by
              one

A GREEN NARRATIVE IN GREEN SHADE

Dylan Thomas's "force that drives the green fuse drives the flower" alludes, at least in part, to the primal energy signified by the Green Man. Thomas portrays the force's potent urgency toward deterioration and death, but the Green Man's energy, even then, despite Thomas's depressive assessment, brims with fecundity. A figure of unlimited vegetative force, the Green Man appears in many cultures and in many disguises. He survives as both pagan god and Christian icon. In the greater archetypes he is the dying and reviving god of ancient religions, and the Sacred Tree as depicted in the Vedas and in Norse mythology. One can catch a glimpse of him, not yet quite overcome by green, in Neolithic imagery, in Tammuz of the Babylonians, in the Egyptian god Osiris, in the Dionysian Mysteries, and in Cernunnos (Kur-noo-nohs) of the Celts. We also sense him in the divinities of Jainism, the American Indian, the Brazilian forest, and in the Aztec God Xipe Tótec (whose "heart is emerald"). He lives in the tales of Robin Hood, Jack-in-the-Green, the King of May, and *Sir Gawain and the Green Knight*.

The Green Man's fertile residence within Christian iconography concentrates, as in no other mythology or religion, in the figure's head. In the West, the oldest type manifests as a single leaf or many leaves forming a male head. In another, vegetation disgorges from his mouth, and even sometimes from his ears and eyes—forming his hair, beard, eyebrows, and moustache. Finally, in some, his face materializes as fruit or flower born and nestled within the green. His eyes always look at us from the original spring.

For me, the Green Man lives most in the Sufi being, Khidr (a wali, or enlightened one, sometime called a prophet or even an angel), known as the Verdant or Green One, whose footsteps leave a green imprint. He appears unexpectedly to the true aspirant and inspired poets when they least expect him and most need him. Khidr, in my opinion, is in all probability the strongest influence on our most familiar church images of the Green Man. After the conquest in the West, Arabic masons and carvers shared not only their highly evolved technical skills, but also their stories, with Romanesque and Gothic artists. Present before then in western culture, the Green Man, at this point, solidifies his power as Christian icon. As a symbol of resurrection and regeneration his image becomes integral, especially from the 11th to the 16th centuries, to many of the great cathedrals and wayside churches of Europe.

The Green Man is not separate from us; he is our source, emphasizing and celebrating the positive creative laws of Nature, the native intelligence that shepherds and protects this world, and the ecological rightness that guides us. The Green Man reveals and bestows life's mysteries—indeed, he embodies them—generating in us the impulse to personify anything that deeply moves us, and compelling us to plow our hands into the soil where his promise dwells, nestled in Persephone's arms, perpetually ready to germinate in and nurture the world.

BITTER HONEY

My summer sweet sweat

The Challenge

Shall I tell the tale from the beginning
Love's human face tendered by ache
Timbers falling
Great grief took me felled me
Shall I tell of Dark Dionysius

Shall I tell the tale over waters
Unfathomable waters not telling
Celestial bowl vessel oceanic
Eros rising masculine movement
Great grief took me felled me
Shall I tell of Dark Dionysius

On one side he who acts
On the other that which undergoes
On one side that never telling
On the other that which tells and never is
Great grief took me felled me
Shall I tell of Dark Dionysius

A buck stomps at wood's edge
Trebling light-hearted wind
Snorting clouds in cool fog's morning
Ferns exhilarating their spore
Great grief took me felled me
I tell of Dark Dionysius

I Am Convinced

After Rilke

I have hit upon
a compromise with my great longing
I am convinced
patience is always good
Nothing that in the deepest sense is justified
in happening
              can remain
unhappened
But now no poetry in me
Only paraphrase

What	*will I do*
Where	*will I go*
Whose name	*will I say*
What breath	*will I feel*

I have hit	Patience

I am	Convinced

Adam's Gospel

Torso trunk tree

Eden's Tattoo

Fearless confident confidences
A few inches of skin

Life story perfect home

SWEAT

Odor first mystified by sun

The Anointing

I would scream yet my tongue a rose in cool milk

SUN

Invite the sun:
Red morning's garment
Bird restorer

To survive
          The sun's pass
          The lightning's strike
          The deluge
          Sulfur rain bitumen rain

When I got home
Self-song
Transparency   Form
Compassionate wings

ORPHEUS

I told the birds
My song's a
pyre fit for love

Only the phoenix believed me

WHAT IS HIDDEN FROM YOU I WILL REVEAL TO YOU*

All love all light all right

*Gospel of Mary Magdalene

BEND IN THE ROAD

No matter how I played on the peripheries the word was

INCOHERENCE: THE CROWD

After Valéry

Dazzled by half
Mingling with the vague
Tumult city
Parliaments streets vanishing

I see my way

THE WORLD OF WHAT

What took you to the station
What were you thinking
What did you inherit
What peculiarities did you acknowledge
What should you did you name it
What is cleverness
What urgency became you

THE LONGING:
LOST MAGNIFICENCE FOUND

After Doris Lessing

Crushing anguish terrible longing
Something out of memory sobbing into exile

One yellow leaf fall
One gold finch startled

I have entered
                    am still within
a room with many doors
landscape before rising sun
quiet flat truthful light

Remove grief:
Put hand in hand

Quiet Storm

In the bunting's blued eye

the enemy
                    the friend

the kiss without within

Pause

before you turn the page

Pause with me ...

There
That's it
The ancient place
The now place

Now go ...

Told in a Dream

My job one raindrop Listen

Poems from The Broken Flower

(2012, Skysill Press)

All Bliss
Consists in this,
To do as Adam did.
Thomas Traherne

Last Born

The sack she prepared
burst under a great weight of bone
I began to sift through pebbles
for my name

The Way it Happened

It began on the roof
He took a broom up the ladder
Started sweeping the debris of three autumns
The wind sound the Dead
removing make-up from their faces
He swept until bugs under pine needles
rode their wings skyward
He a baby
in a crib crying facedown into pillow demons
This poem a black shape
breathing in the straw

CREDO

Now, when I talk
it is not just to say
this or
that.
But it is to say
what is between.

Over there,
under the sycamore, runs
the argumentative
periwinkle.
The blue eye
of southern spring.

Over there,
chickadee whistle
and blue
bird.

Here swings
the blues'
rightful cadence.
Words' melancholic
swarm, thick with
dribble, and
slang.

To my own self
be true.

To say what is
between:
the periwinkle,
the chickadee.

On a Japanese Woodcut:
Woman Looking in a Mirror

After Kitiagwa Utamoro

1

What he sees
in the mirror
is not himself, but
another's image,
lost
looking.

What she sees
in the mirror
is herself,
a Japanese
matron claimed by
pear blossom,
sweet cinnamon.

What he sees in the woodcut
is her seeing,
then,
himself,
again in his mirror.
How like her
he seems.

Nothing is as dark as
he thinks.
The light reflected shapes
thoughts
refracted.

When the mirror reveals him,
a dark man
in a dark time,
with light
shining behind,
he feels the woodcutter
carefully
molding
her face.

2

Oh. So that is what you think?
Tonight stars whirl

in their caves—
eyes sink
to the pool of withering
morning glories.

Are these my hands, the clink
of silver bracelets, mine?
The silken shawl
fallen at the shoulder?
Is that mine, too?

Last night,
among the men,
I left a smoky wave
gathering outside.
I looked.
In the bridge's shadows
I saw,
the cranes.

Take me home, brother.
Winter leaves a feathery sound
blackening my lips.
Tonight I would sleep
under the rain tree's branches,
in a bed
of dry water,
below this
mottled starry cave.

THIS JOURNEY

This a good place
You have come without anything
but the smell
        on your hands
of your suitcase from a previous journey

Perhaps a word   or two
spoken in
        another language
perhaps
        one songbird's tender
mercy under a summer sun

It is a good place   surely
for you are
        here
without malice
        and if   as you think
it must be true:

there is a reason for being here
      whatever it might be
              however
it insinuates itself into you

COMING HOME

Street lights come on.

Not dark
yet,
            but tree-frogs open
their symphonic bags to begin tuning.

When the hooded one stands behind you
tapping his foot to the music
you know you are chosen.
                        He opens the book.
Shows
        you the emblem.
That birth mark on your back.

Suddenly,
            you see everything
            behind you.

A Birthday Valentine: *Althea Rosea*

For Stanley, April 4 and 5, 1992

Would that in this

early April of our births,

the hollyhock, out-

landish rose of the Crusaders,

might guard the garden walk,

in bloom.

Too early for that, but

not for the curled mound

of rich green leaves

precious as their Chinese

and Indian origins.

While the bees sleep

so

do these flowers.

Love comes out

of nowhere, or anywhere,

or every,

and so,

like these mallows,

warm underground

through Winter's wet mess and slump:

my love always.

For summer hides

continually in the leaves,

and at once,

when the sun calls,

opens pink and

singular on the stiff

stalk.

THE ROOM OF THE POET

is like no other room

There gold-beaked birds
sip on remnants of fish
Candles freeze with words
opaque and blue
Armpits glisten with saliva
Fingers remove garments
from the spirit
One by
one

The Sunflowers

All about me people
mingle in and out among the bodies
of themselves and the selves
of others. I wonder how they go
about their business without collapsing,
without their bones breaking
under the knowledge that all
things change. They surprise me
as they move and intertwine
and disintegrate. Something
holds them up. Some glue.
Or miracle. My other tells me
of Faith, the striving
to Perfection leading us.
How together
we will be made
new.
Above,
a sparrow sings with
the tall flowers.

In Praise of Shadows

People say
             we should not linger
with grief
             but bind
instead the bruise
with the future's
             sweet petals

I can't deny that grief's
tentacles
are marine
             carnivorous
but
      in deepest oceans
                          fish
variegate their own lanterns

The amaryllis
             a flower
I have called before
takes to the dark
with vengeance
                  multiplying
scarlet trumpets
when the sun
fills
      finally the kitchen

My God, we leave
behind so much
to gain a little

When
      to go forward
we should only have to
          strike
    a stone for fire
in the wine
cool darkness

THE SEEKER

For Anna Hayes

How long I have been without an answer.

For now,
            I am without one

needing a new acoustic,
                        much time
                        keeping silent.

The deer leap through tall grass:
                                    landlocked dolphins.
The golden empire of the grass.
The deer's telegraphic warning.

As Rilke said:
                    perhaps "mere being
can become an event
                    for us"
so that
            we do not have to move toward it

but through it

(as the deer).

Like the others, I am full
                            as pomegranates
lavishing my rich clay
                        upon the tongue.

Such good odor and miracles
                              bright as flowered bed covers
must await us.

                    But where
the purest air?

With closed eyes we can feel

                              the clouds.
We are all waters,
all unfoldment and melody,
                              stars
revolving in frigid air.

Rilke again:

"We simply *don't know*
what need destroys in a heart,

what it erects."

JOHN THE BAPTIST

The one who comes from above
Is over all
He who is earthly
Belongs to the earth
and speaks to the earth

Gospel of John
(Kalmia Bittleson, translator)

In Andrea del Sarto's painting of Saint John,
the voice crying from the wilderness
is soft and pliant, wreathed by
ivy in the hair—a natural halo.
John's a rugged youth,
splendidly smooth and hard,
draped royally in holy red and brown.
One finger and thumb
from the right hand
point heavenward and to the humble,
thin cross of sticks he carries
for a staff.
Already the fire of Grace
illuminates his face. and the coarse
curls surround him wildly,
umbrous and jungled.
Why does he, then, look down if
not to gaze at earth's lovely darkness
and the water's clear rinse?
For as he points upward, looking
down, the whole story
is told.
The light shining in the darkness, and
the darkness
which cannot hold.

A Stone Falling,
A Falling Stone

I am not afraid to fall.
Drop me from a tower and I
simply hit the earth. Hold on
to me, I am earth still.
I want to fall, it is the first
dream for me. and the earth
my drum that I play.

A stone falling, a falling stone.
Whether I burn or not—
that's beside the point.
The point, this:
when the earth
makes a stone
the sky still fathers it.
When the earth makes a stone,
it's made for falling.

I am not afraid to fall.

THE BROKEN FLOWER

For Alexander Gilmore III

That a broken flower
could speak or

a bird's feather
found forlornly on the path

tell symbols
amazes us.

The last place we would think
to look

there in the discarded
shattered world.

The petals no
less lovely still sing

a loving intention.
The feather a floating

memory forever lightened
by its past.

The hand which carries them
the way humans can

when that which is broken or
displaced is made repaired,

renewed. Rediscovered:
the most perfect flower the most

perfect feather.
That the flower

has no stem only
confirms it.

Oh, and I Thought

1

Oh, and I thought I was special.
It's a game we humans play
to attract your attention. We
think that persistence in
believing it is all for *us*, separately,
will make you come down, cover us like
snow, each chosen, quietly, before the doom
of Death, that close darkness,
takes us up, and Death instead
will be white shadows, and
cold, simple, silence. Instead,
we are meant to learn its
opposite. All together we *are*
special, but separately, *never.*
Spokes in an eternal wheel.

2

I lied before when I said
separately we're not special.
A half-truth at least. Both,
neither/and, we are conflict
impossible to define without
exaggeration or egotism.
In and out of the world
our roles differ, but when
in the world most fully, but
simultaneously, aside, a vibration
begins. A tree bends. The
wind through our branches.
Then. That's the special time.

THE SUICIDE

After Rilke's letters

The open lake,
indescribably open to all.
The dismal background.
This lovely prospect.

Nearly astonished,
I have been ready
to renounce
all its blessings.

Nature, if I am not yet
entirely lost to you:
penetrate
the mind.

Standing
bent
with unrestrainable
heart,

equally difficult,
sullen towards Death:
penetrate
the mind.

AGAINST SORROW

After Rilke's letters

No letter to atone for silence.
          In unison with me,
space untouched,
             angelic space.
Quiet lamps.

                  I am too full.
How I reproach myself,
no longer remaining idle.

I think of you.
                  I have words—
a tree.

    And the poor rain.

I am absorbed,
             altered internally.
A page
        crossed and criss-
                  crossed out.
A future open.
                Infinite
hopelessness cured.

I go out a lot evenings
against the chaos of time.

The maple trees'
            fired leaves.

The Explorer

For Jane Holding's first cast bronze.

In this bronze, a female walks, no tortured Rodin but
Rather the great mother as wiry wisdom woman, primeval,
Striding to gather what she already knows.

Somewhere walking:
                    no
                            somewhere just to *be*

A word spoken:
                    yes
                            perhaps, but also

thought advancing:
                    equine
                    sinewy.

Through life's hollows a
                    civic lesson:
                            the world's rudeness

does not matter—
                    cannot—
                            for the eyes have it:

a world's view of
                    splendor and demise
                            uttered inaudibly

as a walk

                    through leaves:
                                        an autumn sound

breaking
                    making whole:
                                        astonished at

all—
                    by nothing
                                        diminished

Paracelsus::
Concerning the Iris in the Vase

When these varied colors you see,
Persevere. Constantly fan their flame
Until their purple petals consume your cloaked
Distances. The Luna moth will
Lay down her green shawl tonight,
Iridescently white, if you will
Praise this high perfection which
Heals all. Cleanses all.
Whoever always uses this Gilead
Prepares a long fixéd life
Without rust or bruised corruption.
An innocent making and unmaking—
The glass-blower's tincture—
Proving, in fire, the molten lump endures.

TOIL, A DIVINE COMMANDMENT

Sending my body out into the dirt looking
for wheat straw tied to a gospel singer's arm
I met an old woman whose
hair was glowworms and tobacco
She smelled so good I saw figs
ripening early on the bush
I laid my hoe down
singing songs a bullet
sings to a target
I bet my teeth against each turn in the road
An omen took to the wind
I became a scholar of sails
My hoe a wrist in the soil
finding the housekeeper of roots
humming speak to me
Speak
to me

JULY APPLES

My feet
        scorch on the path
A cool spring
        offers its water
The tingling
        goes deeper than skin
It shoots through
the bladder
        into the lungs
I become
        a blow-fish
        green-glistening
I go now
with sure-footed grace
            into the city
to a place
        I recognize
although I do not know
its sound
I can hold
back
no longer
        my hand's
        sparrow movement
        the continual coal
        burning
            inside my living
This tree
whose fruit
        opens a window
into the earth's old voice

The Raising of Lazarus

Lazarus, come forth.
Jesus of Nazareth

A two-fold dying
and then
a two-fold life generated.

This earthly cabinet drawn
towards heat:
its own raw opposite.

The Judah hills return.
The locust tree beside
the cave.

Sparrows smudge
above astonished faces.
Out of that many,

the one
undying redness.
Him.

In the beginning,
a winding sheet.
Olive oil's green odor,

cold.
The infinite instrument,
blinding. and now

these supple
turbulent
thighs

kneeling down.

THE DREAM

They found him in the kitchen
The full moon
beside him with her braided hair
an empty kettle
four stones in a semicircle
on the table

They found a blue word on his tongue
onions in the basket with compasses ready
the frail canopy his blood
bathing his hands
his ten fingers crimped pages
in a book
yellowed
the compasses pointing True North

They found him with my face
and your lips at
the base of his jaw
They found him singing an old song
from the country of crones
about the woods he walked in
when he was young and downy
before he saw

I Have Never Wanted

I have never wanted to
                              write
        the perfect poem, only
the im
                perfect, as the human is
as the stone
                    underfoot's not
            perfect
                            but perfected by its being
stone:
            the poem
                                perfected
by its being
                and me being
            human
                        also that.

I have always wanted the
                                    under
                    side of things, the side
shaded
            by moss, the coolness under
the walkway
                    stone, the silver and
            spotted
                            backside of the *Elaeagnus*
leaf.
        I have
                            always
wanted the elegance
                            of the unseen

when the
          light

first comes through and the shine
                                   was
          (is) there all the time
wanted:

          I have
                    always wanted

the poem
          perfected.

GHAZAL OF LAMENT

I store my words
in great piles of crusty

leaves.
Wait for them to bleat

to open and awaken me.
Enough to have them I tell myself.

Not sell them nor hold them up before
the others.

Sometimes over the ridges crows fly.
My words bluster in the wind

on autumn days.

Moss

Tenderly will I use you curling grass,
It may be you transpire from the breasts of young men.
Walt Whitman

If grass is earth's hair
then this is earth's
                        secret armpit and
            groin—
fleeced and feathered
where musk and dew

augur wind-blown shade

where maleness draws into dirt
                                    and roots tingle
with animosity and grace

Forbidden adhesiveness and merge

        The hair of lovers

A Spell for Poem-Making

A hunger grips my voice
I should not lay it low
Each member has its cry
and I   I move too slow

The rhythms of my heat
The shallows of my arm
Cicadas in sweat-filled air
Tremors of the farm

Confused and like a flame
Wobbling in a breeze
My fragrant voice becomes
A sibilant dis-ease

For everything that moves
I catch the very wind
Sunset in the dogwoods
Southern light within

Could everything but move
Into this steamy light
Provoke my voice its cherubim
Then I could waken night

The chancellor of words
The president of sound

FROM A TRAIN AT DUSK
SOMEWHERE IN VIRGINIA

The armadillos of the sun
make trees into pheasants

Shetlands graze
A cold wind stills the evening

My body sweetens
My spirit's darkened roosters crow

PERSIMMON

For Robert Bell

For about fifty feet above me the straight trunk rises with its scaly square bark. This edge of the field has already turned brown. The first frost and a short autumn rain last week made sure of that. All color has taken to air, splattering the nearby woods with yellow, gold, and ruddy red. Some people call this tree "possumwood" because our nocturnal friend so fondly sleeps in its branches. It's commonly called "persimmon," an old Algonquian name. Its leaves fell earlier.

The limbs splay out, mad and snaky. The sun sinks behind it, and from my footing in the field, it seems a thousand Chinese lanterns light up. "Fruit of the Gods" the Indians called it. Only the virtuous could eat such clean, orange fruit—a defenseless layer of earth's cool breath dusting its flesh. Only a possum dare sleep in such branches.

The loveless have friends in fields with persimmons at the edges, where all loss gathers in burly branches shot through with a natural sorrow. My friend, grandchild of an Indian and a Black, nothing so bleak as bare trees will do for you; but this one, whose laden fruit, warmly colored, sour before frost, wrought with poison, is sweet to the mouth now. The year in ruin. A field never before known. Trembling in silence.

SCORPION

The scorpion on the ledge
does not know what I know

The scorpion on the ledge
has a knife and hole

The scorpion of the ledge
pledges indifference

The scorpion on the ledge
protects from all sorrows

SHADOW

Dear one who lists
me among your treasures

Your shoulders' shy turning
says the gate opens

closes
I am welcome

The path knows your footsteps
When you go out blue

jays rage in judges' coats
You tap your foot

hair stands on end
To fall into you

is to hear rifles
crying

for the heart

LUNCH

Though winter
    sticks in the country's
           heart
plum trees
    bloom in Valence.
           The boy on the train
has his magazines,
    his music, his dreams.
           His mother
nurses her sandwich:
    dry bread and
           polished meat, a simple
lunch.
    Though winter blooms
           in Valence, the mother
languishes:
    her youth used up.
           Her son cloaks
grey eyes
    under her gaze,
           waiting for some-
thing to chew on.
    Taste.
           Something blooming
which he cannot name.

WINTER CEDARS

These solitary things—
                        wretched statues
          fragments
                   of the waxing moon

For all this to happen
                        becoming landscape
myself

            my mouth

in prayer
          To attach myself

ghostly   terrible

                        to the tall cedars

NEW POEMS

Texts from a work-in-progress: Demeter/Persephone
and an unpublished sequence: Gilgamesh/Enkidu

The problem has been to communicate the very spark of life,
and not some opinion about that spark.
Allen Ginsberg

KORE IN THE MEADOWS:
TO THE DAUGHTERS OF OKEANOS

Last night I dreamed of him
He of the ink-dark braids and tattoos
of black fires springing from his groin and brows

He gave me no name
                         only a sinister smoky whirr
murmurings surrounding him
                              as if
whales were calling their mates
                              or rather
              that delicious sizzle
rising up from the meadows
when cicadas lift
              from sleep long underground

I felt his breath hot   humusy with rot
Mineral-full   a rebirthing elixir
His eyes burning topaz radiant
        into my pink sheen

I wanted him!

Have you ever dreamed such a dream
my melodious Sisters, diaphanous Girl Friends?

This morning dew left little freshets
on everything
                  milky-white, making
the fern spores grizzle
                         diamond   *diamond*

Can something so tinsel bear so much meaning?
Is this how night coalesces for dawn?

I am as tender as airborne cottony seed
As golden as bees
Sudden as rain after long drought
Gentle as moss
I drift from flower to grass blade

                                    greener than green

Oh, Sisters, let's go to my favorite meadow
There   over there
I hear there's a new flower

I want to see!

DEMETER TO HECATE

A heart unbroken cannot hold that which cannot be known
Tears fallen unclaimed will not leave your alone
Then alone welcomes you into its whole and populous vacancy

Blue does not blue unless you have been where you would not go
and, when you look with eyes that dare not see
You hear rain
and stars popping wildly in the whiteless night

GILGAMESH/ENKIDU

"I am Enkidu, born in the wilderness." ...

"Enkidu," Gilgamesh breathed. "You have no match, you are mighty as the shooting star of An. I dreamed about you, with none to cut your shaggy hair, born in the wilderness, with none to stand against you." He laid his hand upon Enkidu's shoulder, the warm hide with its soft curls of hair like a pelt of a noble hunting dog, and felt the shaking of the other man's body. For a moment they sat so; then Enkidu surged forward, grasping Gilgamesh hard about the chest so that they lay beating heart to beating heart. Gilgamesh embraced the other in turn, rejoicing in the strength he felt, the strong hard muscles and the clean smell of sweat, Enkidu's body against his own.

"Let us be friends," he said. "There are none as mighty as we in the land, and none to match us save each other."

He would have spoken more, but Enkidu pressed his mouth against his own, his lips soft as the stroking of a duck's wingfeather beneath the hairs of his beard. Gilgamesh felt the blood pounding in his head, his groin swelling hard beneath his kilt to press against Enkidu's thighs." ...

One by one Shamhatu blew out the lamps, her measured tread about the room echoing Gilgamesh's heartbeat, and the heartbeat of Enkidu beneath it. Gilgamesh nuzzled into Enkidu's beard like a lamb into its mother's wool, seeking the sweetness beneath the warm curls, then kissed his lips hungrily until Enkidu's breath came soft and quick against his cheek and he felt the clasp of Enkidu's arms tighten strong about him.

Gilgamesh (version by Stephan Grundy)

This sequence of poems is not a retelling of the myth, but rather a personal response to this story of love, death, and the ecology of outer earth and inner cosmos, the natural world and civilization. Translator Stephen Mitchell says that by the end of the story, "Gilgamesh has become wise. He has absorbed not the conventional wisdom … but the deeper wisdom of the poem's narrative voice, a wisdom that is impartial, humorous, civilized, sexual, irreverent, skeptical of moral absolutes, delighted with the things of this world, and supremely confident in the power of its own language."

Not for the Act Itself but For the Brilliancy it Seeks

Half uttered
                human dark laurel

To live unseen
                I shed flesh

Becoming mind
                I pick harmony

In my breast
                common flesh

Becoming true
                white distances pebbles

"Insignificant" accidents
                restless fire in the rose

Frank calm in footfall

COMPASS ROSE

If they be two, they are two so
As stiff twin compasses are two.
  John Donne

Foot to foot with certain triumph his attention…

Wanted him the green vegetation the fresh air he ran wild…

You see he went on trying with his needle sewing imaginings
                                        and laughter…

Wild neglected garden his black eyelashes his every sleepless hour…

Little dark room on my breast a blush for appearance's sake…

Waiting for nothing moisture dripping you do exist…

Walking in night my manscent hears sound I once could not…

Then we were in space in a spider's web seeing new earth…

ACTION MEN

He wants to know more:
a simplicity:

exhaling the world with stouter
organs longer breaths

There we are:
On-the-spot action men

Near me
your melancholy outpouring

I am above ground again
Even in faint and vague form

The beautiful firmness

Not the least patiently:
your offering

A precious thing:
midsummer coolness

A trumpet note
until the end

The Real Life of a Man Not Known

I saw his cunning but I did not yield
I laughed aloud

He would run until he dropped
all looking at him

He kept his eyes on me
making a low sound suggesting silence

Evening came:
                        the men gone

Again wind
among the boughs   A strange charm

                        in everything

On all physical feats he an oracle a grassy bank
A wooden bench

I thought I had nothing to tell:

We splashed sunlight
The villa's unselfish cameos

When he spoke
                        his arm churned
sun

Too shy to offer me unknown sky:

his lower lip
                    vagrant

He would stand
watching light grow in the stable:
                              a marble horse

combed

                    smooth above the eyes:
feverish brilliant eyes—
                         two

inert fragments of coal

Beside me the sullen determined
                              face

Me defiant
          Momentary

Then shadows fell upon me: a second orange
flash

To want air:
             shade
             bequeathed us

the evening with that odor all
of a shape

Two beasts:
           same blood

humility ordered

compelled exactitude:
                              a living
man

          I dodged that glory:
                                   tall nimbus

All of his might through darkened ozone

Being ruddy flesh he swam
ecstatic silvery centers

Blue-eyed sights

                   In hooded places:

The river rode on

Thermal voices
                            moving them

SAME RIVER TWICE

I could see the city's

                    sleeping gray light
more potent
                closer
by the snowy river

I heard him singing:

His lips
            the river

He slapped his thighs
his metallic muscles
                  an animal

            in a hedge's shade

The road wound among rocks with

        little orchards
        flocks
        white dust tunnels

Everything suddenly restless:

Love's mischief at every turn:

Against the smooth fig
glimmering grotesquely in light

Sobbing:

Make happiness a habit a soft droning

ENKIDU

Something glad and different in his look
watching the lantern enveloping night
bright
        confident
                inquiring

His blue eyes boyish profoundly

Over his token or gesture he's written you
dangerously contagious words

A bull's form disguising the God
Suffering how much to be
                    come so beautiful
So much beauty
           to be
                come the bull

□

A strange sunset came on swiftly
Doused lantern apart in dusk

The Walkup

Faces sabered the shadows
cast through the windows

Streets noises signifying midnight

Someone near me thwacking
the naked street

A faint light
                    fingers out:

silver thread

The Premise

Come see me
We can talk a little
Go straight to the mark
              Blaze my glory paradise
the room into
           relapsing darkness the nevernamed
      thing

◉

First possess him: Slow sand deep spell

◉

He let it in then in every stroke
Marking hours together in his charity
In his effective ferocity

◉

The young man said:

Can a God sleep?

◉

His lips trembling struck dumb hands' unbidden witness

Imminent Flower

From the window the blue
                          jay blurted
out the first thing

So fluid between them:
                          Imminent flower
The only now:
                          The little exasperations:

Very quiet a single
                          lamp burned in
            the hall

His knotted hands
His relenting ribs and chest

Love:

An exhausted but resolving
                          clarity

The blue jay got everything between

        them

The blue jay blurting out the
first thing

Ah!

◻

The whippoorwills stopped

I had sung all night too but

I didn't move at once

EUPHRATES MORNING

Naked men scurrying over stones
Stone wings
Calm pleasure
          Frozen music

I wake to lads
          laughing

CURSE

I see delicate youths made for
                       Love
ordered into Death's engines

Slim youths
           bartered for missiles

Great bull
        God

Make timorous the rude arrogants of the capital

GHOST LOVER ONE

On the lagoon's muddy water:

talking easily with all sorts of men
as though wearied by men's neglect
—lovable, like panic—
he disappeared

The silent house lapped

                         dully at wooden piers

He just hung fire

              Struck
he clung to me

We had air the green door the stucco stained his arrogance

The real exquisite remained: the constant explanation

GHOST LOVER TWO

Its pristine tranquility
                       stood its
final consummation

He
        would shyly reach up
romantically blurring truth
on the inside elbow curve

Some ripple current invited:
live tendrils blackest hair
longing for lost occasions
down to hushed depths

A genius between his shoulders
                             between his hips

If he had never wanted touch he already did

Bath Towel

Besides
      I believe I shall be able

under separate cover
play a few bars on his horn

You Are Never Happy Except When in Motion

He had
      a restless circle
            a moment's stillness

in him
      His long mouth
swelled a face in repose

Mixed sadness and a stone temper
Long arms   meaty legs
His voice pitched
         open plains

The plain type of new lad
Brisk
      Blunt
         Hearty

We left before daylight
         The weather
foul
      speculative

He found his attention its
           Well-guarded interest
washed away by vulnerable swashing echoes

Weeping day lifted a hand to him

He took it
      a dark and half-
         hidden lake
against bulky shores

THAT'S EVERYTHING YOU NEED

He remembered a
                              question

or something around him

Through midnight odor of mountain
between midnight and dawn:
                                        tilted upward

he crouched
                        listening to the forest:

        sibilant disturbed brush
        earth"s understones

A name soft on his tongue:

Low hours
                        now vanished

Massive ridges
blackness greater than before

A lower country:
                                robust

woodsmoke through the door

Across his arm over
                                thigh summits

downslope through the black hill

        creases

THIS RAIN

Singing to himself the coming
                              disasters
autumn rain
                    daylight noises

Reconciled secrecy
                          resentment
Fields desolate

The old man opened his eyes for a moment:

Great Sphinx moths
                            timid
embarrassed

Then I understood
What he heard
What he deduced

Take care
You are lucky

Water singing gently

DARKWOOD

Night in my childhood
                    came strange:
a stick found on the roadside strangeness
of being
              without company

Our house
            facing the stream
                      kind enough

I used to think I saw
                a person
enter the dark wood
                his deep black eyes
an interruption
             among tree tops:
birds singing

He threw gloom
              invigorated air
within one symmetry
                to make me Certain
                in the Wood

When my queer guide parted the bushes
beside the forbidden brook

a single ray
              passing through me
making me start:

At last I met the man

He held a lantern
                    shedding dim light

Long black hair fell upon his shoulders

This is the place he said
I will prepare you

Dazzled
                I saw the features before me were
my own

HUMBABA

But this is not the only reason
You are here
                    Is it

Not far away land
becomes desert

                    Red stones
                    Red dusk

So I rise

Walking

Scrutinizing footsteps in the road

Looking again
on wet trees turning
                    them silver

Walking

Warm gray light
                    across my body

THE EXQUISITE INCIDENT

arrived yesterday

Morning and afternoon:
flawless

It was really the
voice:
           present fury
           felt as need

The rest of it:
              so rare

(Your dangers)

Darkness
          hard won

Storm over

           Clouds
                  Creamy-colored

Pale blue sky

AFTERIMAGE

The problem has been to communicate the very spark of life,
and not some opinion about that spark.
Allen Ginsberg

DIVERSION ON A BIRTHDAY

For Stanley, 1995

> *There is no excellent beauty that hath*
> *not some strangeness in the proportion.*
> Sir Walter Raleigh

A little:
       This hedge
whole
          unto which
                 Green
may deliver you

Through the arches
                 Lustre
Health
       and Sweetness

Because of going wet
                 no foulness
so fish may be kept

The blackbird
         for cleanly
innocently

Bees
   to love
               to become
thriving in our orchard

What spring-like murmurings

What summer grasshoppers

The small owl astonished
                              now
in the blackberries

Within the boxwood maze
light from behind
                              The new sprigs
their young leaves
                              virginal
golden-green like
                              bees

Air
          mild and modest
Love
          fearlessly
                    complexly

Bringing forth fruit
                    fresh cuttings
                              from vines
the honest corn
               Fields
interspersed with thickets
                              dizzying
The kiss
          extremely always

GRATEFUL ACKNOWLEDGEMENT is made to the editors and publishers in whose publications some of these poems appeared. For acknowledgements of pre-book publication of poems in *The Golden Legend*, *Midwinter Fires*, *Submergences*, *Visions of Dame Kind*, *Gospel Earth*, and *The Broken Flower* please see those individual volumes. After publication of many of these books, including *The Beautiful Tendons*, poems have appeared in the chapbook *On Hounded Ground*, and in the magazines and anthologies *Assaracus*, *Collective Brightness*, *Gay City*, *My Laureate's Lasso*, *The Light in Ordinary Things*, *Madder Love: Queer Men in the Precincts of Surrealism*, and *North Carolina on 9/11*. I am grateful to those editors for those later publications. Some of the poems from *The Broken Flower* and *Gospel Earth* were featured in an exhibition of my poetry and photographs "Not What It Seems," photographs and poems at Through This Lens Gallery, in Durham, North Carolina. Three poems from *The Beautiful Tendons* were formed into a cantata "Heaven's Birds: Lament and Song: A Cantata for World AIDS Day," arranged and composed by Steven Serpa, performed and published by the composer, Boston: MA, (December 1, 2009).

"Demeter to Hecate"—*Simple Vows Anthology* and The Jargon Society web site *Musings for the Season*. Part of "The Premise," part of "Enkidu" (with the title "Minos"), "A strange sunset," "The whippoorwills stopped," and "Curse," originally appeared in a booklet entitled *Me Moving* from Longhouse Publishers and Booksellers. Thank you to choreographer Natasa Trifan for using text from the minotaur poems in a dance piece, *Somewhere Towards the Center*, with her Natasa Trifan Performance Group.

Many of the poems, except those of *Gospel Earth*, *Demeter/Persephone*, and *Gilgamesh/Enkidu*, can be heard on the 2 CD collection *What We Have Lost: New and Selected Poems 1977–2001* (Green Finch Press, 2002).

I am indebted to those reviewers and other journalists, bloggers, and readers who spread the word about the first edition of this book. Two radio interviews should be mentioned: NPR's Frank Stasio *The State of Things* on WUNC FM Radio, and Asheville's community radio WPVM 103.5 FM Word-Play with Jeff Davis. Links to both interviews can be found on my web site. The first edition was recommended by the American Library Association Gay, Lesbian, Bisexual & Transgendered Round Table for libraries that have a GLBT or modern poetry collection and was an Amazon.com "Body Electric pick" from the Body Electric School (San Diego, CA). Notoriously a poor stay-at-home poet, the publication also led to visits to the 2008 Atlanta Queer Literary Festival, the 2009 first annual GALLA (Gay and Lesbian Literary Arts Festival, Stonewall Archives, Fort Lauderdale), as the keynote speaker at Ferrum College's (Virginia) 2008 Arts and Humanities Conference "Gender Roles in a Shrinking World", and numerous readings across North Carolina. Thank you to all.

The poems in the original *Tendons* appeared previously in: Alpha Beat Press's *Alpha Beat Soup* chaplet series in *Jeffery Beam's Allnatural Heatsensitive Ganeshapproved Zuppapoetic Alphabeat Spiritibody Soup, Amethyst, Asheville Poetry Review, Aura, Bay Windows, Black Men/White Men Anthology, Brightleaf: A Southern Review of Books, Cairn, Carolina Spring, Catalyst, The Catalyst (UNC-CH), Clown War, Evergreen Chronicles, Faultlines, Four Zoas Night House Anthology, The Front Page, Gargyole, Gay City II, Gay Sunshine, Gay Sunshine Fiction Anthology, Gay Roots, Green Finch Keenings, Hummingbird, The Hague Review, The Harvard Gay and Lesbian Review, The Independent Weekly, The James White Review, The Jargon Society web site Musings for the Season,*

Kiss of the Whip, Lambda Newsletter, Lilliput Review, Lodestar Quarterly, Madder Love: Queer Men in the Precincts of Surrealism, Main Street Rag, modern words, Mouth of the Dragon, A Murder of Crows, Nantahala Review, Off the Rocks, Oyster Boy Review, Parada równosci :antologia wspólczesnej amerykanskiej poezji gejowskiej I lesbijskiej (Rainbow Parade: Anthology of Contemporary American Gay and Lesbian Poetry), The Poet Cannot Contain Himself, Poetry Salzburg Review, Provincetown Arts, Sanskrit, Success!—Chimera: I Am My Own Twin, The Sun, Tobacco Road, Yellow Silk, Yellow Silk Anthology, and *Wolfpen Branch.* "Angel" originally appeared in *Hummingbird* as "On the Rocks." "The Spell" originally appeared in *The Fountain*; "His Penis" originally appeared in *Submergences*, "Medieval Song," "Qasida of Your Presence," "Where Runs the Sap," and an earlier version of "Lament" originally appeared in *Two Preludes for the Beautiful*. A number of these poems were used in a theatrical performance, *Let the Crooked Flower Speak: A Poetic Autobiography*, at Manbites Dog Theater, Durham, North Carolina, 1994. "Von Gloeden" was presented in its entirety at the Modern Museum in Durham, North Carolina in connection with an exhibition of visual art inspired by the photographs of Von Gloeden, 1996. A number of these poems can be heard on the 2 CD collection *What We Have Lost: New and Selected Poems 1977–2001* (Green Finch Press, 2002), including sung versions of "Variation on a Malay Theme," "The Spirit of Forms," "Troubadour Song," "Medieval Song," "Tomorrow he comes," and "Qasida of Your Presence." The introductory essay, "The Visionary Company of Love," originally appeared in the Self Knowledge Symposium's magazine *The Symposium*, vol. 3 no. 2, October 2000, and reprinted in *White Crane Journal*, no 51 (Intention) Winter 2001 /2002. It has been revised slightly.

It was also excerpted in *Charmed Lives: Gay Spirit in Story-telling* edited by Toby Johnson and Steve Berman, volume 1 of the White Crane Wisdom Series, 2006.

My deepest gratitude to the reviewers and publications who commented on the first edition of *The Beautiful Tendons*.

The excerpt from the legend of Gilgamesh and Enkidu is from Stephan Grundy's version: *Gilgamesh*, NY: William Morrow (an imprint of HarperCollins Publishers), ©2000 by Stephan Grundy and Melodi Lammond Grundy. I am also indebted to the Stephen Mitchell version of this legendary epic, and his brilliant introduction and notes which accompany it.

Jeffery Beam: A Bibliography

The Golden Legend (Floating Island Publications)

Two Preludes for the Beautiful (Universal)

Midwinter Fires (French Broad Press)

The Fountain (NC Wesleyan College Press)

Submergences (Off the Cuff Books)

Light and Shadow: The Photographs of Claire Yaffa (Aperture)

little (diminishing books/Green Finch Press)

Visions of Dame Kind (The Jargon Society)

An Elizabethan Bestiary: Retold (Horse and Buggy Press)

What We Have Lost: New and Selected Poems 1977-2001
(Green Finch Press)
[A spoken word/multimedia 2 CD collection]

Life of the Bee (Rock Valley Music)
[Libretto for a song cycle by Lee Hoiby]

New Growth—Shauna Holiman and Friends:
New Songs and Spoken Poems
(Albany Records)
[A CD collection including Life of the Bee]

Old Sunflower, You Bowed to No One: Poet Lorine Niedecker
[Special supplement to Oyster Boy Review]

GOSPEL EARTH AND GOSPEL EARTH II
(LONGHOUSE PUBLISHERS AND BOOKSELLERS)
[TWO CHAPLET SELECTIONS AND AN ONLINE CHAPBOOK]

ON HOUNDED GROUND: HOME AND THE CREATIVE LIFE
(BOOKGIRL PRESS, JAPAN)

THE BEAUTIFUL TENDONS: UNCOLLECTED QUEER POEMS 1969-2007
(WHITE CRANE BOOKS)

A HORNET'S NEST
(THE JARGON SOCIETY/GREEN FINCH PRESS)
[COMPILER/EDITOR—A JONATHAN WILLIAMS QUOTE BOOK]

HEAVEN'S BIRDS: LAMENT AND SONG
[LIBRETTO FOR A CANTATA BY STEVEN SERPA]

AN INVOCATION (COUNTRY VALLEY PRESS)
[LIMITED EDITION CHAPBOOK]

ME MOVING (LONGHOUSE PUBLISHERS AND BOOKSELLERS)

GOSPEL EARTH (SKYSILL PRESS)

MountSeaEden (CHESTER CREEK PRESS)
[LETTERPRESS LIMITED EDITION]

MIDWINTER FIRES
(SEVEN KITCHENS PRESS REBOUND SERIES)
[A NEW EDITION WITH A NEW INTRODUCTION BY JOE DONAHUE]

THE BROKEN FLOWER: POEMS (SKYSILL PRESS)

THE LORD OF ORCHARDS: JONATHAN WILLIAMS AT 80
[ONLINE FEATURE JACKET MAGAZINE—CO-EDITED WITH RICHARD OWENS]

BLUE DARTER—JONATHAN WILLIAMS:
A BIBLIOGRAPHY OF THE PUBLICATIONS AND EPHEMERA 1950-2008
[IN PROGRESS]

FAMILY SECRETS
A JAKE HEGGIE SONG-CYCLE FOR SOPRANO ANDREA MOORE
WITH ALLAN GURGANUS, RANDALL KENAN, MICHAEL MALONE,
LEE SMITH, DANIEL WALLACE
[IN PROGRESS]

SIX METAMORPHOSES AFTER BRITTEN'S OVID
[IN PROGRESS—LIBRETTO FOR STEVEN SERPA]

JEFFERY BEAM is the author of numerous works of poetry and song as listed on the pages previous. His work was surveyed in *Literary Trails of North Carolina*, Duke University's Rainbow Triangle Oral History Project, and in Greenwood Press's *Contemporary Gay American Poets and Playwrights: An A-Z Guide*, *Encyclopedia of Contemporary LGBTQ Literature of the United States*, and *Lesbian Gay Bisexual Transgendered Queer America Today Encyclopedia*. He is currently at work on a number of projects including a song cycle with Steven Serpa inspired by Benjamin Britten's *Six Metamorphoses after Ovid*, an opera libretto based on the Demeter / Persephone myth, *The Life of the Bee*, *They Say: A Commonplace Book on Poetry and the Spirit*, and a series of illustrated children's books. Beam appeared in 2002 at Carnegie Hall to read his *Life of the Bee* poems for the premiere performance of Lee Hoiby's *Life of the Bee* song-cycle. The cycle continues to be performed on the national and international stage. Beam's poems have appeared in innumerable magazines and his essays and criticism have appeared in many publications including *The Advocate*, *The American Book Review*, *The Christian Science Monitor*, *Contemporary Gay American Poets and Playwrights*, *Big Bridge*, *Encyclopedia of Contemporary LGBTQ Literature of the United States*, *Encyclopedia of North Carolina*, *Garden Design*, *The Harvard Gay and Lesbian Review*, *Lambda Book Report*, *Contemporary Gay American*

Poets and Playwrights: An A-Z Guide, Lesbian Gay Bisexual Transgendered Queer America Today Encyclopedia, The North Carolina Literary Review, Rain Taxi, Small Press Review, Smithsonian, The Sun, Yellow Silk, and *Oyster Boy Review.* His works have received numerous awards and grants including four American Library Association Notable Book and Gay / Lesbian Non-fiction Award nominations, two Pushcart nominations, an IPPY Ten Best Books Award, an Audie Award, an AIGA 50 Best Books Award, a Writer's Digest Editor award for best E-Zine poetry outlet, a North Carolina Writers Network Blumenthal Writers and Readers Award, a Nazim Hikmet Poetry Festival award, a Chapel Hill Transit/ *Carolina Quarterly* Bards on the Bus award, a Durham Arts Council Emerging Artist Grant, a Duke University *Chronicle* award, a Provost Award for Public Service from the UNC-Chapel Hill Center for Public Service, and a grant from the Mary Duke Biddle Foundation. His papers are on deposit in the North Carolina Writers Collection, Manuscripts Department, University of North Carolina at Chapel Hill. Born and raised in Kannapolis, North Carolina, Jeffery lives in Hillsborough, NC with his partner of 33 years, Stanley Finch. He serves as poetry editor for *Oyster Boy Review.* He recently retired from his position as the Assistant to the Biology Librarian in the Botany Library at the University of North Carolina at Chapel Hill. At UNC he also penned "Song of the University Worker" which was recently designated the official staff poem. For ten years he served as a judge for the Lambda Book Awards. You can read and hear more of his poetry at his web site: http://www.unc.edu/~jeffbeam/index.html

S P U Y T E N   D U Y V I L
Meeting Eyes Bindery
Triton
Lithic Scatter

A WORLD OF NOTHING BUT NATIONS   Tod Thilleman
A WORLD OF NOTHING BUT SELF-INFLICTION   Tod Thilleman
WRECKAGE OF REASON   (ed.) Nava Renek
XIAN DYAD   Jason Price Everett
The YELLOW HOUSE   Robin Behn
YOU, ME, AND THE INSECTS   Barbara Henning